Austin's Indigenous Offspring

by Zell Miller III

Released April 2026

Printed in the United States of America
Cover Photo Roj Rodriguez
Edited by Michael Whalen, Sunni Soper
ISBN 979-8-9880540-4-7
Published by 310 Brown Street
www.310brownstreet.com

Austin Indigenous Offspring is my debut that arrives already rooted—listening to the ground before it speaks. In this first collection, I tried to write Austin not as postcard or punchline, but as a living body shaped by memory, resistance, joy, and contradiction. These poems move through neighborhoods and bloodlines, stages and sidewalks, asking who gets to belong, who gets erased, and what it means to claim home in a city constantly remaking itself.

The title *Austin Indigenous Offspring* originates from my one-man show, *Chronicles of an Indigenous Offspring*, and stands as a deliberate homage to **Notes of a Native Son** by **James Baldwin**, whose work reshaped how personal history and cultural critique can coexist on the page. In this context, "indigenous" is used specifically to describe my lived experience of growing up in Austin—formed by the city's rhythms, contradictions, and creative lineage. It is not intended to speak for, replace, or appropriate the Indigenous tribes whose histories in Austin have been systematically erased, but rather to acknowledge a personal, place-based inheritance shaped by environment and community. Hip-hop culture is paramount to my work and serves as both a formal and philosophical backbone of the collection. The poems move with the sensibilities of hip-hop—sampling memory, looping refrains, bending language through rhythm, breath, and emphasis. Hip-hop functions here not simply as influence, but as methodology: a way of telling truth, preserving stories, and resisting erasure. It shapes how the poems sound, how they move on the page, and how they demand to be heard aloud. In this way, my writing aligns with hip-hop's tradition of turning lived experience into archive, performance into testimony. I hope my voice is intimate and communal at once: a poet bearing witness while calling others into the circle. The work honors ancestry—artistic, cultural, and chosen—while insisting on the present moment, where identity is negotiated daily through language, love, labor, and loss. Music, theater, and the cadence of spoken word pulse beneath the lines, giving the collection an oral history feel, as if each poem were meant to be shared aloud and carried forward. The uses of slashes are not only here to capture the rhythm of the language, but its also a dedication Ntozake Shange's Broadway play "forcoloredgirlswhoconsidersuicidewhentherainbowisenuf". This play changed my perspective on writing and performing. This book is not only an introduction to a poet, but a declaration of presence. *Austin Indigenous Offspring* asserts that the stories born of this place—especially those shaped by marginalized voices, are not footnotes to the city's narrative; they are its heartbeat. This book is dedicated to my parents, Zell and Vernell Miller (rest in power momma), my big brother Keith DeShay (rest in power) and my mentor Laurie Carlos (rest in power). To Ashley Miller, the love of my life, and my two greatest creations, Zell IV and Marley, big bro Tony and baby sis Robbie. Shout out to Mike Whalen for early editing, Dr. Omi for the love.

Peace and blessings.

Zell Miller III

With *Austin's Indigenous Offspring*, Zell Miller III has crafted his own Spirit-filled, genre-bending artform. Flavored with jazz and hip-hop impulses, shaped by the words of James Baldwin and the Love of Laurie Carlos, fed by a family that helped him know he could be a writer—an exceptional writer—Zell takes the reader through a dense complex universe. The work is a tender, uniquely unflinching homage to family, neighborhood, mentors, Blackness and an Austin that is no more. Beyond the nostalgia that some of us feel about the vibrant, quirky, often brilliant theatre scene of bygone times, or the sense of possibility that just seemed to be in the air—Zell names the pernicious racism, the prescient middle school theatre teachers, the sturdy allies across thorny divides, *and the steadfast familial truths that permeated his world*—a world that told him he was capable of anything. With a deft hand for repetition, a sonic acuity that prods the reader to speak the text out loud, and the seasoned flow of someone who has written for the page *and* the stage, Zell has done his family—and those of us who knew Black Austin—proud. This is the first book from a writer who has many more books to offer.

Omi Osun Joni L. Jones
Author of *Theatrical Jazz: Performance, Àṣẹ, and the Power of the Present Moment* (University of Ohio Press, 2015)

Professor Emerita, African and African Diaspora Studies Department
University of Texas at Austin

Zell Miller III

Singers of the Daybreak… I See U

Table of Contents

Mic Check 1… Mic Check 2

I do this / 4 those brown and Black babies / who get a maybe

while children with less melanin / get a guaranteed yes

I do this / because the Goddess chose I / 2 rain words from the sky

2 blow holes / through these baseless / stereotypical shows

I do this / 4 the beat riders / the graffiti artists / the DJs / and the breakers

minus the misogyny

I do this 4 Ida B. Wells / 4 Laurie Carlos / 4 Nikki Giovanni

4 Malcolm X / 4 James Baldwin / 4 Amiri Baraka / 4 Ta-Nehisi Coates

I write or I die

this is 4 the memory of my mother / Vernell

and those yellow brick projects of my youth

this is 4 Ashley / 4 Marley / 4 Zell the 4th

4 Brian Keith DeShay rest in power / 4 Robbie / 4 Tony

and all my nephews and nieces

this is 4 / the thousands of youths / I have taught

2 pick up a pen / and spit they truth

taught them / 2 talk they shit / in open spaces / minus their background

Nas said / all we need is one mic

I sent one prayer / with one poem /

Goddess please / I hope I did it right

from a DaShade / 2 a Cora Lee / 2 once T-fly now standing as a BLakchyl

I do this 4 my father / who openly took that sacrifice

so I wouldn't have 2 pay the price / but for his labor

the bill has come due / Austin, Tx / pay me what u owe

and as Lauryn Hill said

and even after all my logic and my theory

I add a "Motherfucker"

so U ignant niggas

hear me

Zell Miller III

Refugee… Me? 1st Movement
(from the play *Echo of a Refugee… Me?*)

I am a Black artist voice

and these buildings / are covering up the sky

to where I can no longer see / the blue in it

so my heart / just hums them now

the blues

I am the intersection / crossed out

I am

The disproportionate / disappearing

Once was / me

I am……………………………………gone.

Zell Miller III

In a Semi-Half Circle

In a semi-half circle / blue bulbs provide electric light / incense on the ceiling

indigenous style in my approach / what's native 2 me is my tongue / familiar subject matters keep me focused / lord knows through these current political times

I have been forced into ADD / attention deficiency dominates / scripture

says nothing 2 me / is that the problem / in trying 2 get closer to God / I listen to beats

by T-Man / he is the son of a minister like I am

the son of God / but I'm holy no longer

feeling kinda hereticish / remembering my beginnings / 1142 Mercer Drive

Apartment 108 / remembering kissing bony Nessa under a cardboard box / remembering how I woke up with a scar on my forehead / mother smoking Viceroys / my daddy smoking Kools / and I had asthma / dig it / see caught up in the contradictions / I wanted 2 get closer to God so I invited Them to dinner / but they sent Kahlil Gibran instead / we sat on softwood floors / and ate circle food ontriangle plates / he brought greens / they were sweet like ambrosia / Kahlil was good company / we had conversations without words / we debated in magenta for hours / he rolled ginger root in soft leaves / and never asked me 2 take a toke

I still wanted to see God / ask them about this Lucifer thang / see dig it / 2 me

God is omnipotent / I mean don't nothing go down without Their knowledge right

so / what could reverberate in Satan's ear to make him
challenge God / U think Satan don't weep

every day / U think he don't pray every day / he is just being a
good vessel

like we all should

this was God's right-hand man / see it's not Satan we should B
hating

it's his disciples / that's how the so-called devil can sit next 2 U
in church / wearing a dress / and pants / I confess I'm in love
with love / I want 2 provide truth sermons / 4 those whose
conditions / have been conditioned / in a semi-half circle

I sling automatic weapons / verbally click my GLOCK / and
rock the cradles of toy made MCs I refuse 2 battle poets / Y
waste time / pissed at the slams / well slams

R the will of the people like mumble rap my will is in court
awaiting sentencing / see it's trying 2 get free / trying 2 listen 4
God / wondering will They speak through water / but I was
told our egos prevent us from hearing the voice of God

but God gave us ego / and vanity / it's all from the same
source / and energy locks in my hair and

makes my teeth quake / in a semi-half circle I stand incomplete

not a full 360 / like our bibles and other religious books / so
I'm trusting only in my

beliefs / and they reshape hourly / like postmodern drawings /
sirens explode the night adjustments to light / once in the dark
/ can B painful / and I walked in the dark 4 so long

no mo tho

moving with purpose / and the secrets sit on the dollar bill / 13

steps like there are 13 in the images / once U believe that
now you're on the Road to Enlightenment

Zell Miller III

Speaking the Spoken with Broken English
(from the play *Chronicles of an Indigenous Offspring*)

I am the writer rewritten

I'm singing syncopated salutations

I'm spitting sensational symbolism

I'm operating organizational order

I am brilliantly bringing / bountiful blessings /

see / son of man / see son of a goddess

see son of a gun / the firing pin / it B my tongue

I inhale your gentrification / and when I exhale / that's when I get mean

That's why I treat these lines / like M16s

1 click of the tongue / I let loose the hammer

I bump stock my poetry / then I Ra ra ra ra ra ra tat rapid fire

5.56 caliber grammar

streets sound like 808 bass drums

pushed by corner blockers / who bleed blocks

then bleed on blocks

who try 2 clock the digital decibels

but fall off / cause the rhythmic metronome

bounces 2 a different frequency

2 free the MCs / who stumble on the good foot

but falls on the one / the big bad wolf /

he ain't your enemy dun / it's some of these pork products in badges

that keep our neighborhoods outlined in chalk

then they try to stalk / the Black brown / who try to make mounds

from the / straws and sticks found

but when you build your house out of bricks

that's when it gets thick / that's when they bounce with rapid release speed

in a so-called effort 2 / keep the peace

it's these hopes and clues / that keeps us singing the blues

that's got us / so confused / on how the line / it keeps getting moved

see this is post / 1928 grand master plan

read your real history on Austin, Texas / and see how they legally

lynched Black homeowners / and took their land

and read the deep histories of / zilker park / pease park / and barton springs

and I just want 2 know / when the gates get locked / or come undone

how R we always on the outside son

Zell Miller III

this b / that spoken broken / vehicular homicide ish

we R loading rounds and clips of truth

we doing drive byes

we R aiming right at these myths / and historians

the mission is to uncover the secret pathways

so we can bring about better now a days

don't hold the truth like you held us in bondage

set it free and let's see where it lands

we know in these trump and jd vance times

your designs / R the total eradication / and erasure

of my kind / and we know that saying goodbye to our babies / could literally be the last time

cause they are hunted in these streets / by some of your badge-wearing beasts

so / don't talk to me about double standards / or fair exchange

cause freedom and equality / were never the mission

in those documents / your ancestors made

but what do I know

I am just the writer rewritten my nigga

I'm singing syncopated salutations

I'm spitting sensational symbolism

I'm operating organizational order

I am brilliantly bringing / bountiful blessings /

see / son of man / see son of a goddess

see son of a gun / the firing pin / it B my tongue

I inhale your gentrification / and when I exhale / that's when I get mean

That's why I treat these lines/ like M16s

1 click of the tongue / I let loose the hammer

I bump stock my poetry / then I Ra ra ra ra ra ra tat rapid fire

5.56 caliber grammar

And I am aiming them right at you Austin, Texas

click,

click,

click

BANG!

Zell Miller III

B: A Meditation on 2 Thyself for Marley

B / a meditation on 2 thyself / B / the 2nd letter of the alphabet

a verb

a noun

a system

a process

a reminder when things get heavy / or heated / u can just / B

U can B in the space between it all / don't B afraid 2 take a breath / before U speak / but

remember / no matter what comes out of your mouth / U must always

B / unapologetically U / stand firm in the belief / U / R not alone

U / R a piece of the universal jigsaw puzzle / waiting 2 B found

trust the universe / she will always find U / B present in the real / reality

B clear / U / R needed / U / R loved / U matter

and all we will ever ask of U / is U / B yourself / so U might as well

B

but / if that is 2 much in the moment / then we want U to take permission / 2 not

B

and we will honor that / but U can

B loud / B sad

B broken / B happy / B confused / B excited

B the beat / B the second beat

2 somebody's heartbeat / B calm / B terrified / B bold

B the reason they speak of people who look like U / in glowing terms

B free of negativity / rise above it

B the boom and the bap / B the kick and the drum

B the guitar / and the solo / B the bass / and the line

B the body politic / stand on both sides of the aisle

B a pronoun / or not

B your dreams / and not somebody's vision 4 U

B the vessel / and the spirit / and the push / 4 yourself first

then blast that energy into the world

B the basketball bounced / and the ankles breaking

B the sound and the fury / of teen existence

B your own high five / dance when the world is singing / stand up

and speak out / against violence / done to those who walk in the shadows

B open to new experiences

B unapologetically U

B the 1 who stands up / and says / "Free Palestine!"

B the boss / and

B the labor

B brazen / and

B weak

B the singular sensational somebody / who helped somebody singularly sensational

make it to the next moment

and when U have done all U can do

when U have said all U can say

and the Moon decides to shine

then we need U 2 B gone

B rested

B dream-filled

B still

B recharged

because when the Sun decides to smile

then we need U 2 B up

we need U 2 B willing

we need U 2 B ready for the fight

Because

U

beloved

U deserved it

because U were hand picked

hand-selected by the creator-ess

God

and

God B A

Woman

placed here in this moment

at this time

so your light can illuminate our future

we need U 2 B here and not gone by your own hand

we need U 2 B

we need U 2 B

B: it's a meditation on2 thyself

Zell Miller III

B: it's a mediation on2 thyself

B: it's the second letter of the alphabet

a noun / a verb / a process / a reminder

B: it's a meditation

a mediation

a medication

a ___________

Zell Miller III

Eyes of Fallen Genius
for Miguel Piñero and Jean-Michel Basquiat

Eyes of fallen genius

it's 3:00 a.m. / under a full Moon

this is where the poets dwell

there are these secret conversations happening

that no one hears, but God

consciousness is an extension or the pure, unfiltered translation of God

and I find myself

looking behind at a long night / and thinking ahead to an even longer day

but the seduction of silence

the 4biddenness of it all

shit

nigga can't help but be intrigued, yaknow, seduced by the sexiness,

yaknow, the idea of spirit speaking just for you / to translate

it's 3:00 a.m. / under a full Moon

and I wouldn't know sleep even it kissed me deep and wet

tongue tight / and offered herself to me completely

I long for the noise / the busyness of a home / where a 4-year-old rules,

but this right here / this quiet

brings visions of dreams

I never knew they were not the same

visions / and dreams

until then

until now

I remember to be surprised by their entrance

I catch a moving one by the front of its breath / and I am moving

light speed

wishing for the ability

to hear with Miguel Piñero's ears

Rican / and junkie

genius / and madness

I wanna hear them

talking

hear them in a muffled conversation / until I can't take no more

until I need to put a needle filled with death in every vein

until the veins become to 2 small / and I find myself in a mirror / drawn out

strung out

Zell Miller III

out

out there on the edge of reality / floating in 0 gravity

unshaved and unbathed / in some junkie hold-up / hanging out

etching my manuscript in the ears of the fallen / too brave to be heroes

I wanna hear children

speaking in broken English / and Spanglish / clapping out beats

with feet / and smiling in the heat / that burns like the center of my palm

hot from the ideas that brew and stew in me

shit

I wanna hear Hollywood calling

Broadway begging

then I wanna hear the sound of broken dreams, as they splash against the window of my reality / and when death comes knocking / I will escort them cats in / cause the wind will whisper my name / and the sand will hold

and move me through time and space / and shit / every now and then

give me the opportunity to blow across the bosom and cheek / of some whore

who whores / for reasons that could be fixed with government programs but she caught in the bam / and boom / won't let her groove / and body rocking mocking drum machines / won't let us soothe / have to keep that body popping baby

yeah

it's 3:00 a.m. / under a watchful eye of a full Moon

I consume the space

like she

we hover long / shifting focus

my daughter / sleeps

strong / and long

in dreams I have missed out on

it's 3:00 a.m. / under a full Moon

I pray to

see strong / with the eyes of Jean-Michel Basquiat

it's the winter of my descent

cold blazed in blue / I gather / unlike the hunter

boxed in cardboard

middle-class upbringing

but the world never looks

quite like I see it

crafting the graffiti in street terms

Zell Miller III

the words of modern times critics / stirs / and burns

I bask in every area code / but no one hears me

the trustees are blocking my path

they won't let me leave

I am my own oppression

white powder burned to liquid gold

goal being

straight to the soul / and my sole lingers

and I see / see strong and long / see / all this against the N.Y. skyline

like Jean-Michel

a target for the pen / who never wanted the Black hand in

I see the daggers in the faces / and places

I leave the traces of my pain tattooed to the skin

my skin

again

and

again

I am

akin

"graffiti will never B art" in the eyes of a vast minority parts

they come

they come

and I came

all over their daughters' sheets / how is it / that I'm not supposed to weep

my mother's voice bounces off the bells

I hear them 2 well

see too many of her in these N.Y. streets

that's all I have ever tried to do / was speak

for those who can't

seem to get it in synch / but the timing always falters

then fails

the trustees

are bothering me

they won't let me

sleep

won't let me sleep

the trustees

are at my door

again

it's 3:00 a.m. and this is where poets live to die

and be reborn

Zell Miller III

again

and / again

and / again

Zell Miller III

My Love Supreme in A Minor
for Ashley Miller

tell me of the many moons constructed / that were inspired by your smile

tell me of the thousands of sunsets / that R mere reflections of your eyes

we dance in free verse / we talk in constructed movement

when you are near / catch me

there

hovering

right about boiling

that is how you leave me / when you enter the room

one would believe / you enter to an orchestrated progression

lead by violins and cellos / as a child of the 70s / me

that was the soundtrack of the heart / but u didn't enter to that composition

no / my love /there R no strings

like Peter Brady when he saw Kerry Hathaway

nope / no strings like when Lionel Jefferson saw Jenny Willis

no / when I see / saw U

my heart sings of deep-seated southern 808 bass drums

with trippy hi hats / and Bootsy Collins astro bass lines

Dig / I'm talkingbout

stanky southern fried funk

produced by Dungeon Family head / Rico Wade

hard hitting shit like that

Yeah / we talkingbout

DRUMS

when you announce yourself

as quietly as you think you do

I hear pounding drums

perfected percussive passages

yeah

when I see your face / and those eyes

I hear congas / bongos / timbales / claves / maracas / cowbells

all moving in a spinning / magical motion / vibrating

and all turned past 10 / like when you are talking to family members

and your accent pushes through

the volume of your beauty is deafening

Zell Miller III

and I would gladly lose hearing and all senses / for one single kiss

In my mind / U pounce in open gaps and spaces / catch all parts of my soul

as ancient as dreams untold

hands and arms needing to fill U in them / and then I want to

fold into you / like warm towels out of the dryer

nuzzle into flawless creases and precision

by hands of mothers on a Sunday afternoon

U B a pineapple upside down cake

birthday wishes / no misses / but proud to be my misses

you wear our love / like your favorite Frida Kahlo shirt

it's comfortable / Like our love

U / mi corazon / U

singing Kahlo quotes / in quarter-notes

Frida hummed in perfect pitch key / you now repeat to me

quote / "Feet, what do I need you for / when I have wings to fly?"

I love 2 escape in corners 2 create consecrated caresses

we hold hands like old couples

and kiss like high school kids / aware of the significance

of every moment granted that shall not be taken / but this foundation of us

is rock solid / tell me of the salty air whispered by the ocean

and the prepossessing landscapes of your homeland Puerto Rico

Ashley, my love

I have been anticipating U / like Christmas morning rituals as a child

and if U know me / U would truly know how deep that is / ask my brother Tony

baby

U B the Tom Browne Jamaica Funk played at 10 and repeat / on a boiling hot summer night under a Texas sky

U B that first chill / then comfort / of the first dive into Northwest pool on July 4th

like our love / our respect and trust seem to expand way past the due dates

our love is written in hieroglyphics / on the walls of both Egyptian

and that other side of U / the Mayan pyramids

tell me of the bittersweet taste of 2nd chances

asked if I would do it all over again to be here / yes / could not come fast enough

Zell Miller III

we had to go through our own private Hells / to be here

in this everlasting / and waking to you / is still my favorite verb

this

is not love

this is living / this is the whispers of poets / the vision of artists

the hope of the heart / unbroken / this is the / CAN'T BELIEVE U EXIST

all the tears have dried / and my Sunday morning worship service

U r the being of light so perfect / cutting through

and I am the receiver / and the promise of together

tell me of our connection / closer than the break of the breath

born between the patterns / there is always the truth and that is us / united

Zell Miller III

I Wonder

I wonder / what would happen

if we supported dreamers / and our youth

past the age of 18 / I wonder / If we told our young voices

yes / all things are possible / and had financial support

behind those mystical magical words to support that thought

I wonder / if we could mean it / when we say to them

there are no limitations to what you can accomplish

if we / as a community / a country / a society

devalued wealth / and material possessions

if we actually / fostered that child-like spirit of play

cause given the chance / children don't see differences

until we tell them they are there / but / if we focus our energy

less on the players / and more on the lessons from the games

what would our country feel like / if our vocabulary changed

and the narrative was rewritten / instead saying I / we chose to rock with we / and / instead of teaching our girls / not to get raped

we taught our boys / not to rape / what if we taught our boys

how to take rejection / instilled in them confidence so when they heard no / it wasn't an indictment on their character / it didn't

crash their whole world / what if we taught boys / you are not promised just because you are a boy / and phrases like

you throw like a girl / became positive affirmation / and what
if we taught / gender has multi-boxes / more than just the two

and you have a right / to be your true self / and your true
gender / or neither / and whatever it is / because really / it is
your business / and not the government / or your neighbors /
what if we taught

when a child is conceived / the women who are carrying / have
the right and control over their bodies / and nobody /
including doctors / religious folk / politicians / have a right to
tell them anything / what if we learned how to / agree to
disagree / and not attack each other

over the disagreement / I wonder what it would look like

if we could agree / there is one true living God

but They are multilingual / and multiracial / and bigger than
any religious book can capture / understood all prayers are
honored

and those who choose not to believe

are treated with the same respect / as those who do

I wonder what our country would sound like

if sports teams / didn't demean / and degrade entire cultures

what if / we valued education / like we value sports
competitions

and tens of thousands of people / crowded coliseums and
stadiums

to hear debates / or spelling bees / or math Olympics / or
science fairs

Zell Miller III

or / poetry slams / or one-act plays / what if we tried / to offer arts programming / for everyone / not just those who can afford them

what if we gave our educators / the same hero-worship / we do our sports

and / entertainment figures / what if / we paid them sports and entertainment figures / what would these united spaces taste like

if we allowed dreamers / and youth / to mature to visionaries / and planners / what if we stopped / with the bitter back and forth / to each other / what if political parties didn't even matter / that we vote for the person / who is going to help us the most / what if we praised and cared for the land / the water / and the air / like we praise over-priced cars

and clothes / and things we never really needed

and maybe nature / wouldn't rise / spin / drench / and fight back

so hard and so strong against / us

what if education / wasn't still to this day / segregated

if we protected our dreamers and youth / what if we didn't allow them to be killed in school settings / that we agree personal protection or hunting is a right / but owning military-style guns is outlawed / for civilians and cops / what if we all agreed / reparations are due

but let's start with the heart / and an apology and actually mean it

then our country could be safe / there will be no need

to make it great again / if we stood up and spoke out

against those who would harm / if we shunned those who would disrespect women / if we stopped chasing our own image

on social media / and valued ourselves / for ourselves / and not

by how many likes we get / if we held each other accountable / for the pain we leave behind / can you imagine / if all this was a reality / then there would never be a reason to utter the phrases, "Free at last. Free at last. Thank God almighty, we are free at last." / "Make some good trouble" / or "Our body, our choice" / or "Black lives matter" because

in this alterative

u-n-I-verse / the constitution wouldn't be written by rich white men who wore wigs and blouses and stockings / those same men would later B worshipped in this country but / trans or LGBTQ+IA young people are demonized for how they dress / or express themselves / imagine that world just for a second / then take a breath / and in your mind's eye ask yourself / what are U doing / to bring that to a reality

She Like a Jazz Drummer Solo
for Marley

She like a jazz drummer solo

in synch with the universal order

spins with elegant grace

full and fast

laughs with her head back

mouth open

like a Charlie Brown comic strip

my baby girl shines

she shines / speaks with syncopated brilliance of a 88-key jazzologist

she my sax solo

eyes always on me

When she don't listen / don't get her way

she sandstorms the pyramids with fit / and clenched fist and foot stomp

try to door slam and

My voice RAISE / and her chin becomes attached to her chest

But we talk through / mistakes / teachable times

Hugs like an anaconda

2 tight sometimes / to where I can't take a step

Cause she wrapped herself all around my leg

We plug tuning with beat

De La / she my Soul / sound sunny weather

When inclement weather approaching

She grinning with full smile and entire body

She spinning / spin / turn / fall / and repeat cycle

See me cleaning / she want to assist / in all areas / but she room

She boot in living room / and boot in bathroom

But never she closet

She loud laughs till she cough

Till she wheezing / till she throws up

And laugh again

She is the never-ending cycle of joy

Fashion conscious

Change clothes / 5 times a day if I let her

She like a jazz drummer solo / in synch with the universal order / spins with the elegant grace / full and fast / laughs with her mouth open / like a Charlie Brown comic strip

my baby girl shines

Precious cargo

She be my intricate pattern / rhythm ride

Zell Miller III

Rolling

She like a jazz drummer / not even Sun can match she
energy / she extends
And she be / me / mine / morning glowing
Funny face focused / genius / burning bright
Bunny bouncing born / and me / I be Dada
And loving her / way past my extended lifetime warranty
is over.

Zell Miller III

A Black Mother's Hum at Midnight

my momma was worried 4 me

cause in this country

they crown Black kings / who have the audacity 2 dream

did you think U were Martin? / With those ears of Lawrence

you should have been heard / when U come from meager means

who do U think U R / what gives U the right to think U could / ever/ try to climb

Everest / they would rather have U

laid out / legs spread in your driveway / like a Medgar Evers /

my momma was worried 4 me / when you step into the area of discourse

they have no choice / when your voice is sublimed / and then aligned /

with purpose / when you can uncover the covered truths /

they put an X on your chest / and leave U like Betty

Malcolm less / yeah /

my momma was worried 4 me

as my foot pushed past broken glass /

peeping them as they stalk / slide right past the broken

sidewalks

I / Arthur / Xcaliber / with this pen / I thee wed / at the edge

ain't no turning back / times Sun / times Moon / equals me / chilling

at 90 degrees / my breath is not a given / ancestor aching / Armageddon

in the namesake / eyes with more clarity / watch words like spirits

actions speak with better volume / life is not promised

so each one / teach multitudes / the pen is lighter than a TEC-9 /

so it's easier to conceal / but the damage be the same sign

9 B a non-prime number / numerology

is just another division / in trying to get closer to the higher self

7 signs track the wicked / post office these demons / with letter bombs

resurrected and free / mirror only reflects the God in me /

I am the resurrected rise / speak like lyrical lighting

illuminating the night / then catchphrases filled philosophies

uncharted genius / that's the James Baldwin in he / born beautifully brilliant

beginning / Sun-kissed by God / with a tongue torn with truth

emancipate the proclamation / hand it back to the youth

third day theory / 7th day sought / pain in the residue of multicolored hues

dead books and Sunday gatherings / but they still don't take their shoes off

on holy / sacred land / once walked by Egyptians and Aesop the only fable

is he was / white / but he is all African / but I B / son of man / lost in the wilderness

seeking / we speak in broken beats / graffiti like a tattooed tongue

windmill to catch my spirit / use my phalanges / to paint better degrees

this ain't no 33 degrees / it's decreed by the hand / holy man / Heaven-sent angel

in benevolence but / you let the promise of riches and gold change you / bury me

because of my beginnings / then change the rules when you see fit

know who is really sinning /

my momma was worried 4 me

cause in this country / they crown Black kings / who have the audacity 2 dream

who did you think U R / Martin? / With those ears of Lawrence

you should have been heard / that when U come from meager means who do U think U R /

that's why /

my momma was worried 4 me.

Zell Miller III

We the People for the A-Town

It's simple / right

3 words

It's the vision of Martin Luther King's dream

the one he spoke about in the capital city of Washington, D.C.

in 1963

3 words

We the people

All of us / humans / minus race / creed / color or / gender

minus sexual orientation / economic conditions /

we talking bout / all of us / here in Austin / and all her surrounding

sisters and brothers

all of us / on every corner / and block / in this weird city of ours

3 words

We the people

Like

I love U

Simple / to the point

But clenched-fist strong

3 words

We the people

And / like that clenched fist / those three words

can be thrown / with the force of a bare-knuckle gut punch

Leaving the / one on the other end

Breathless / spinning / trying to find balance

That's how I felt / the first time / I held my son

3 words

holding my first born

standing in St. David's Hospital / downtown / Austin

standing with my back to the room / holding my son

standing looking out of a gigantic window

standing / holding my son / that gigantic window looks /

small when it comes / to the love I have for him

standing holding my son / in downtown Austin / I wanted to show him / the Austin skyline

the Moon on one side / and the Sun on the other / it was one of those bright beautiful Austin days / August 25th, 1999

That simple skyline of 25 years ago is gone

what could be traced with a finger

now today needs a full hand

3 words

We the people

Zell Miller III

we are as diverse as snowflakes

when band together / we can make storms / drown out the political lines that dominate our daily lives / together we can

use the force of our collective winds

to push back /against the wall of supremacy / now towering in our view

we the people

when melted / we can be what John Lewis said /

make some good trouble / we can be the waters to topple this madness around us

But we must link together

and

In unison / we can rise above / the muck and clogs

of these grotesque abuses of power

but only as

We the people

in my weird little city of Austin with our small-town charm,

but big-city problems

protest is served like mouthwatering brisket from Sam's Bar-B-Que

on 12th street

3 words

We the people

I may not be LGBTQ+IA,

but I know I stand right there by their side / 10 toes down

like I'm not Latinx / or Asian / or Palestinian / or Irish / or Jewish /

or Middle Eastern /

but I know if I don't stand now

there will be no one left to stand for me / in this city of mine

Austin / so proud to be

the blue dot in the center of the red state / of Texas

in my city / histories / get painted over with fresh coats of white paint

and pretty strokes

but look close enough / those racial bruises

Don't Come Clean

even when u rub them with coco-butter cream

but on these Austin streets / of my city

I am the prime example of what happens

when cultures clash and become / 3 words

We   the   people

it was a Jewish theater owner on 4th street Michel Jaroschy

and a white middle school theater teacher / at Dobie Middle School

Mr. Jerry Miller / who helped a Black kid from a strong Black family growing in an Austin housing project / Springdale Gardens / in East Austin / find his way to the stage / where he would ultimately / find himself

and it was a Latinx reading teacher Mrs. Rosette / and Black English teacher Mr. Harris / 7th grade / and another Black male English teacher

Mr. Nolan / 8th grade / who gave that same Black boy the tools of words /and how to use to them /

combined with the work ethic of his parents / Zell, Jr. and Vernell /

who were able to purchase their first home / on the north side of the city

those teachers gave him the books / and permission and the

yellow brick road / to push himself / and find the wizard /

to bring pens to bleed

blue and black ink / all over white pages / where he would inspire

young poets / and artists / and one day / stand as the

inaugural Poet Laureate of Austin, Tx / it was those books

that inspired him / from authors like Baldwin / that is James /

Giovanni / that is Nikki / Blake / that is William /

and Langston to the Hughes and an Edgar Allan who is Poe /

they taught me

that I could also paint words to mirror

the summer sunsets on Congress Avenue / so in love with my

city

that sings the blues / in hues of deep purples and cotton candy skies

it's so easy to get lost in the rich rolling waters / named for the freedom fighting Lady Bird / her lake manifest dreamy / sweet sticky

summer days and nights / Austin / a crown chipped / but still sparkles with the collective brilliance / under our constant Sun / till the clouds make waves / then back again / the constant about our weather /

is it will change / without a moment's notice / cept / for the summer singe of the yellow rays / for days / in the pockets of certain sections /

of the city / some areas where the landscape of the residents have shifted or been erased / it's these moments that makes my city / unbearable / yes, weird / and beautiful

and frustrating/ and charming

but none of it can stand / if not for the 3 words

We the people

Powerful and simple and true

That is how we overcome /

We the people

Simple / Right?

Zell Miller III

Springdale Gardens 1142 Mercer Drive Nothing Ever Better (Nothing Ever Better)

In the orbit of my youth. Floating through that existence in this galaxy called Austin, I was the 3rd planet from my mom and dad's sun. Two bigger planets before me. We shall call them Keith and Tony. Then the 4th planet exploded into our galaxy. A little girl named Robbie. I find focus, with a multiverse if you will. Where I grew up, on the east side of this constellation, our world consisted of 6 to 8 square blocks. I loved it. I know when you tell certain people you grew up in a housing project, they make assumptions. Not out loud, but you see the look on their faces. Worse, they give you pity pout. But in our house, or apartment in Springdale Gardens 1142 Mercer Drive, Apartment 108, there was joy! A childhood for the ages. I never thought about being poor, cause in my little 4-, 5-, 6-year-old brain, we weren't. I could see the difference between us and lots of our neighbors. My father and mother made sure we were always good at the cost of sleep for themselves. They worked multiple jobs, which meant, in a 2 parent home sometimes, 3 to 4 checks were cashed, and none of them came from the government. We had new clothes, our own beds, toys, but this is the early-to-mid-70s. Our imagination was so much better than toys. We had a huge crew of neighborhood friends. We never missed meals. Sadly, some of our friends did. My parents had a sweet, green Pontiac LaMans with whitewall tires and super white interior. We had a hi-fi, and a color TV. We even had a set of play clothes and shoes. We had it all. We had a giant pecan tree we could climb and get a snack from. We had a dried-out creek that served as the central character in all kinds of adventures. We had a slab of concrete that doubled as a basketball court and a clothesline. We had an entire community that looked out for each other. Sometimes a little too much. There was no need for pagers or cell phones. Naa. Someone heard you say something or do something wrong and by the time you tried to beat that ghetto hotline home, there was my mommie standing on our little front stoop ready to greet you with belt in hand? We didn't think about being Black, because everyone around us was. I mean different shades and what not, but everyone was Black. There was no need to be told to walk with pride. We did it, cause we saw our fathers and mothers doing it. My mother was a coffee-colored Black woman, when you put two creams and two sugars in it. She was a short woman in stature, but her presence was always felt before she even entered a room. My mom had the demeanor of a prison warden, but a cool one, not like white men in the 70s flicks, you know, "What we have here is a failure to communicate." Instead, "I'm gonna ask you one more time and, if you lie, then I'm not responsible for what happens to you." She was fair, I can say that, as long as you kept it moving, did what you were told, she let you make it; but get out of line, and she reminded you quickly of where that line started and ended. She had a gold crown on her front tooth and an afro. She always had this devilish kinda grin, and when she widened that grin and you saw that gold crown, you knew you were in the presence of a gangsta. Is that Black enough for you? She never raised her voice and rarely repeated herself. She would laugh from the side of her mouth, and it was clear she was Captain Kirk on this Starship Enterprise. Rare was the moment you didn't find her without a cigarette from her right hand and a bottle of Pepsi in her left. My dad was straight up out of a comic book (Marvel, not DC): short in frame, his skin tone was coffee with cream and sugar muscles on top of muscles. I mean, I think even his toenails had muscles. Kept his hair in a flat top, In my mind, Luke Cage couldn't fuck with my pops! He was the real Power Man. A multi-gold glove champ, he moved with that fighter swag. So, if you didn't know him and you saw him coming towards you, then you got out of his way, but the people who knew him, knew he would do anything, anytime, anywhere to help. When he wasn't working, he was always clean. For the white people in the back, that means he was always dressed nice. Everybody loved my dad, and when he smiled, with his Kool cigarette hanging out the right side of his mouth, holding his Schlitz malt liquor, he made your whole soul happy. I always knew we were a little bit different, because in every other house in that complex, there was a picture of white Jesus, and Martin Luther King, Jr hanging in the kitchen. My momma said "I will never have a picture of white jesus, cause it's a lie. Jesus was black and MLK, cheated on his wife and he was an asshole for letting children get attacked by dogs, and water hoses, but what really made me mad was when they would let those children get arrested to fill up jails, what kind shit is that? They are kids. Grown people should have done better." Is that Black enough for you? She once told me, "I wanted to hang a picture of Malcom X, because I liked a lot of what he was talking about. I think Black and white should have stayed separated. Once we started integrating, it killed all the Black businesses and, beside that, Malcolm X was fine! He had that cute smile, but he was too skinny for me. You know them Black Muslims don't eat meat." I had never really heard anyone refer to the honorable Malcom X as fine. She said, "Now who I didn't like that little creepy Elijah Muhummad. He was like most leaders: using God to get what he wanted." She would say "I'll tell you this: don't believe anything you read, because every book was written by man, and man is a liar!" She laughed, "I really wouldn't feel good about hanging up Malcolm in the house, because I like pork chops way too much to be looking at him while I'm eating. This is my house? Who the Hell is he?" We had no idea what our parents were facing once they docked their spaceships in other parts of the galaxy called Austin. You see, in the multiverse you have to be able to give up who you are in your world so that version of you could operate in that world cause they knew that world better. Once we left our world, we were now aliens. I loved the me I was on our home planet, and I refused to allow any other version of me to exist. That caused a lot of problems at my school, Sims Elementary. My kindergarten was fine, but my 1st grade teacher was a young white woman, who wasn't ready for me to be my Springdale self. So, we clashed all the time. When it was time to venture out, like on Saturdays, or when my momma had errands, we all had to go. That was tough for me, because I didn't get along with that version of my mom. Once when we landed our spaceship at some store or place of business, her devilish grin became a fake smile, her speech patterns were flavorless, and she was very different from my cigarette-smoking, Pepsi-drinking, profanity-mouthed momma of Springdale Gardens. And the rules: don't touch nothing, don't talk to nobody unless they talk to you, and, when they do, you say *yes sir*, *no ma'am*, keep your hands in your pockets, don't make them think you took something, don't touch each other, keep your voices down. As a child, I just thought we did something wrong, she had no patience. As a grown man, she was protecting us from being blamed for something. Looking back, it was the mid 70s. She was just a few years from 1964 when the manager of the Woolworth's Downtown Austin told her to "Keep your black ass off my building. I don't want your nigger color messing up my bricks." That's Austin, Tx. We weren't aware of the pressure she was under, to break those images of us white people had put into her psyche. The pressure to be a Black woman was even more because, as a mother, you know you have to protect your kids. Nobody would be able to say her children weren't behaved. She would not allow us to be the images they had laid out on how we acted, how we smelled, how we talked. I guess she didn't realize it wasn't them who were harming us, but it was her and her expectations. There was no book for this shit. The shadow of whiteness loomed large, and this version of my momma thought this was the best way to handle it. I still didn't really get it till later, how oppression can change your thought patterns directly or indirectly. I call it 2nd hand racism, like 2nd hand smoke. It may not kill you, but it's just as deadly.

Singers of the Daybreak… I See U

We b

singing for the daybreak / but never see the dawn

2 the beat boom knockers / street poets who get put on pause

2 the streets drenched with crimson liquid of dark skin people

2 the silence that shatters from a mother's moan

2 the gut wrenching cries of a father screaming / *"burn this bitch down"* / after the murderers of his son go free

2 the empty chair at breakfast

2 the black president who didn't say or do too much / would it have been different if he had sons

2 the officer who knows the truth / but can't speak on it

cause they stand behind that blue wall

2 the childhood dreams turned adult nightmares

I see U

2 the 10 eyes that will never lay them on their fallen father 2 the spots on the walls where diplomas will never hang

2 the cigarettes unsold

2 the skittles uneaten

2 the cigarillos unsmoked / don't matter if they were stolen or paid 4

2 the iced tea unopened / the bullets still fired / the morality of a nation still unchecked

2 U / and the conversations you will never have 2 have / this is

2 U

2 the dreamers shot with reality

2 the bible thumpers who teach hate

2 the poets who write about murder / but do nothing in the community / the hip-hoppers hoping the internet will crash / the billionaires who profit from pain

I see U

the caged bird who gladly wears the shackles

2 the community activist who controls their partner

2 U who hears that crash next door / but says it's not my business

2 the child who witnesses then repeats

2 the child who witnesses / and refuses 2 repeat

2 the wife of the murderer / who now questions everything / about her badge-wearing spouse

2 the sleepless nights brought on by the missing / the beds that will never again B laid in / the caskets / the lies they tell / the prosecutor who plays defense attorney / still looking for a

reason / Y a grand jury had 2 interview U
for 4 hours / Officer Wilson
2 U

I see U
I see U

U are seen

and 1 day
justice will B done

Zell Miller III

Look What God Made
for Robbie (Baby Sis)

a brilliant person is described as / "one who is exceptionally clever

intelligent / skillful / quick thinking / and possessing keen problem-solving abilities"

my sister is the walking representation of brilliance

shining / she beams brighter than the Sun / she B

a Godly woman / she also got that Springdale Gardens eastside

pumping in her blood / U would not want 2 try it / I suggest / U tread lightly

she walks with faith / never tap dancing on the spaces between

I say she is brilliant / because I witnessed her / transform into a wife/ a mother

an award-winning educator / and through it all / never once did she compromise

who she is / she stands in mirror reflection of proverbs 31:25

"She is clothed with strength and dignity; she can laugh at the days to come."

that is my sister / never lowering herself / or bowing her head to anyone

but her God / never shying away from the positive / I have

never known a stronger person than she / a once super talented gymnast / U never / wanted to see her in a 50-yard dash / girl or boy / her heart is my favorite part of her / bigger than all oceans combined / tender with her teachings / had all her babies reading before they started school / firm in her stance for foolishness / known on her campus as Mrs. Mac / close my eyes and I would have never dreamed / this baby girl

with a room full of dolls / a quick wit / and strong right hook / I had to block a few of those growing up / who would have believed / she would become one of my best friends / as siblings we feuded / sometimes worse than

the Hatfields and McCoys / nowadays it's over Hook 'Em Horns / or Boomer Sooners

she is always on time with her morning prayers / because of her strength

and dignity / she understands that patience is a virtue / and sometimes the best way to teach is to model the practice of listening / my sister continues to B

the fashionista / shoe game is sicker than a beef recall / and she makes miracles happen with her teaching acumen and god-given skills / I am in awe / I stay in honor / and stand strong / as her brother / her laugh can still bring the joy of fireflies on a June night on Dallum Dr. / her encouragement is legendary / never more than a phone call away / I thank the creator daily for blessing me with yes / the world's greatest / smartest / stylish / amazing sister / a brilliant person is described as "one who is exceptionally clever / intelligent / skillful / quick thinking / and possessing keen problem-solving abilities / all of that is my sister / clothed in her strength and dignity she who

Zell Miller III

dances in the center of love / she B / beaming / brighter than the Sun / she B my sister / Robbie Lynn Miller-McClendon / and I am a better man

father / husband / artist / human being / because of who she is / and has always been

Zell Miller III

Once They Placed U in My Hands
for the Virgo, 08/25/99

Once they placed U in my hands

all attempts at anticipation were out

U / entered into this world / with Orpheus / intent

in the fact / U / demanded to be heard

the nurse station froze for several seconds

1 nurse was quoted as saying /

"*I have never heard a child sound like that*"

and she was right / eyes closed / U fought through your entrance into this world

knowing the quiet times of intergalactic serenity

Once they placed U in my hands / I could no longer hold

so dear to me / the twisted metallic cutting views on race

I was embarrassed by my hate / so much so / it took days

to look U in the eyes / in a quiet room while your mother slept

U rested in my arms / U stirred weak from your journey / this little being

defined perfection / born on a full moon / in my hands

I felt the ultra-magnetics align for this brief moment / in my hands

Once they placed U in my hands / I could not see U in me / but U saw me in U

hands held in fists / tight stance / ready to rebel / ain't been here a full hour

my son smiled within his first minute/ knowing U now

I think it was just a warning for me / of what U have in store for me

long sleepless nights / long afternoons / of chasing U from room to room

but knowing these times can't be lived again / so we squeeze

each moment 4 what it's worth / holding U in my hands / knowing U hail

from Mercury / I see the fire in your left eyebrow U arch it like an arrow

like your old man / same antisocial behavior

U will have to work through that, baby boy / I held U above my head

and U extended your arms and feet in flight position

I see this is not a new position 4 U / my son grips his rattle with his left hand

and researches faces in crowds and marks them friend or foe

Once they placed U in my arms the world became a free freedom ringing

Zell Miller III

in the mirrored ancestral voices of the great tribal dancers / and warriors

I hold U close to my chest / cause that's where U were searching for warmth

that day / your first day / and I'm here to give it son / I will love U

with every follicle in my hair / to the very skin on the bottom of my feet

Once they placed U in my arms / I tasted air and understood the meaning

of love / and with that I can never question the concept / or belief of faith

Once they placed U in my arms / I heard God and it was the soul dance

I searched for so long

thank you son

and I love U

thank U for making me a better me

Zell Miller III

The Vastness of Knowing Love

I.

Bare naked in the ocean / did I ever tell U / U R my ocean floor

I walk in awe of your ability 2 harmonize / with nature

I'm able 2 / breathe on dry land / cause of U / mermaid with attitude

save me from myself / you're a perfect being of light / transmit 2 me

from the center of Earth / your cool quiet tantalizing pleasure

like a Hershey's bar on Christmas morning / you are the hazard of being free

down rainy streets / your conversation never changes / U don't raise your voice

above the rain / that would be disrespectful / we R sharing

eggrolls in noisy restaurants on crowded streets / where we find each other

time and time again / U / R picking shells of sand / running through your fingers

quiet when the tide comes calling / at night / you are the reason the Moon glows in my eyes / I bet if U wanted 2 / U could capsize existence / how do U pray

is it mumbles / or hushes / or screams / or songs / birth tones with words 2 combine

rhythms / I'm stark in comparison 2 U / bare naked in the ocean

U
complete
me

Zell Miller III

II.

Bare naked in Sunshine / shall I conceal my purpose / 4 this visit

there is a lick I'm trying 2 get 2 / *hello kitty* / warm embraces and traces

of sacred steps 2 honor ancestors / will U allow me 2 dip my finger into

the ocean represented in the depth of your brown eyes / how dare U come

crashing into my open window / did I scream that loud with my broken heart

did U know that I ache 4 U / in misty tones that convert themselves into

excuses 2 work late / trying not 2 tempt fate / but I'm already lost in U

U R the coming of greatness / has anyone ever beheld your eyes like me

in this moment / right now / I asked not out of curiosity / but out of wonderment

I'm lost within the slender / caress of your walk

it was the sexy cut of your legs that brought me to this state / my ears are rattling

from the absolute freedom of your laugh / come pray with me angel / help me

translate the late night symphony / will U play 4 me / your smile is the rainbow

and I pretend / not 2 feel pain / bare naked in Sunshine

U

complete me

Zell Miller III

III.

Bare naked in streets / I'm the corner holder / saggy-pants protester

checking 4 patterns of walking perfection / and there U B / smiling with chants

brought 2 U by your native lands / Latin ever since / U B / San Juan beaches and Mexico City coolness / Look at U / smiling with chants brought 2 U / courtesy of the rain / I wanna walk with U / dig / has anyone every told U / that U / R / the lick of a jazz tune / U / B bright brass / and sculpted ebony and ivory keys / banging when U work them eyes that way / arched eyebrows / a warning of sensational nights I'm ready / 2 kiss U like a freed slave / kisses his freed ground

I'm caught

trapped between quarter-notes / been watching / U walk this way 4 some time now

shall I speak / what do U say to an Angel / *"hey"*

no answer

that's cool, I'm let U walk on

shit

she stopped

now what?

I want 2 just say/ I just want 2 B around U

I don't care where U R / If you are in the grocery store / I just want 2 B

in the next aisle over / If U R at the movie theater / I just want 2 B 2 or 3 seats over

If U R at a red light / can I B in the next lane / but by the way U drive

I'd just rather wait on U / at the next stop / and embrace that face

I got a mental photo of U / pouring warm liquids over ice in solid glasses

your fuel 4 the day / I pray your fingers stir the combination / so I can overdose

on your sweetness / bare naked in streets

U complete me

Zell Miller III

Suicide Note for the colored girls who keep pushing through, praying the rainbow is enuf. please know u r seen and heard and believed.
(from the play *Ballot Eats the Bullet*)

This would be my suicide note / found in the back pocket of my favorite jeans / ink still fresh / and a little smudged / these words have come together in protest / but peacefully assembled / they may remind one of a dream / an idea / a plan to be free a political party moving as a single unit / a perfect union / separated by imaginary lines / and boundaries / and secrets / and lies / and violence / just like america / my soul stirs and shakes / I sometimes cringe at brown paper bags / thinking sister / this is how we determined who could enter the room / if your skin tone was darker than a brown paper bag / you may not be able to sit with us / sistas / how did we end up here / we made our own jim crow laws / and I'm just so tired / I can't go another day walking on this soil / see my soul / my soul / can't take another day / this would be my suicide note found in the back pocket / of my favorite jeans / those jeans / that took a whole minute to find / cause no one is checking for us / designers don't make jeans to properly fit / it's either they fit fine in the front / but not the back / or you have too much room in the back / and the front is awkward / and if hidden cameras were in the dressing room / it would look like a wrestling match / cause I'm supposed to just fit into your society / right / never mind my curves / my sanity/ my power / my magic / I'm just supposed to play by your rules / and I'm just tired / I'm tired of wearing the mask / fake smiling to get through the day / to make you feel comfortable / lest the myth of the angry black woman be real / well I'm tired of apologizing / so fuck you / cause I am angry / there is every reason in the world for that anger to be justified / cause you keep killing my brothas / my sistas / my children / my husbands / my fathers / my mothers / and I'm so muthafucking tired / and none of the officers ever go to jail / there is always a justification / but you didn't kill the white man who killed two people in San Antonio / then came to Austin / shot two cops / killed 4 other people / why is it us who only get killed / and why do we have to say / Black Lives Matter / cause throughout the history of this country / you by your actions keep telling us they don't / and so how am I supposed to feel / how am I supposed to function knowing my children don't matter in your eyes / so yes / this is my suicide note found in the back pocket of my favorite jeans / written in black ink / written with a pen left / by a student / not even a favorite student / not a student you would notice if she was missing / just unassuming / respectful / quiet / doesn't cause any problems / wouldn't notice her in the halls / she is beautiful / but you wouldn't notice if you never noticed her / big brown eyes / wanted to stay after and ask me about college / whose face / I will never forget / ever / she wanted to talk about the lack of Black women in the history books / like how 3 Black women Mary Johnson / Katherine Johnson and / Dorothy Vaughan / helped america get to the Moon / or Henrietta Lack whose cells were stolen and they helped to fight cancer / and other diseases like polio and HIV / and how this one student / was really smart/ great at math / but a white female teacher told her / to be an engineer / she would have to go to a really good school / and that really good schools / cost a lot of money / even after a scholarship / it would be very expensive / so she was thinking of doing something different / didn't want to be a burden on anyone / and in her / I saw myself / and sometimes the struggle is just too damn real / she said her joy was in solving mathematical problems / and at that moment / I couldn't tell her where my joy was hiding / cause I'm tired / cause the skin I'm in carries too much pressure / cause if you're confident / they hate you for it / but then they tell you you must be strong / well / fuck you / I just want to be / why can't I be like a white man / use the dick between my legs to walk this Earth and exercise my privilege / this baby in front of me should want and achieve everything / but I have nothing to give her in this moment / and that inferno in her / will slowly begin to fade / like mine /

Zell Miller III

cause every day it's a goddamn fight / and nobody is checking for us / 276 Nigerian girls get kidnapped / and the world keeps spinning / let one blonde-haired blue-eyed girl go missing / the world stops / resources are gathered / media is alerted / but for us / nobody is checking for us and today goddamit / I can't take another breath / step / I can't float in this sea of unrest / and attacks on us / just cause we are who we are / I just want to release my breath / close my eyes / and let the undertow take me under / cause love seems to be a social construct / devoid of reality / so I sit in my one-room apartment I can no longer afford / in a city where Black and brown people are continually pushed out to the margins / I can't see the Sun from the new constructions / they will spend multi-millions to build / but there are schools full of Black and brown kids who don't have text books / whose facilities are outdated / how are they supposed to learn / and I can't find my tribe / and lonely is calling me to tongue kiss a razor blade / drink a wine glass full of cyanide / make a noose from my sheets and hang in my closet / walk into traffic / find entry into one of the new high rises and free fall / in my favorite jeans / and they would find this note written in black ink / this is my suicide note / found in the back pocket of my favorite jeans / cause I'm tired / and I think of Nina Simone / standing on a stage in France / past her point / playing to pay her bills / 300 dollars a night / and that ball of confusion circling in her stomach / spinning with hurricane force into rage / and they question why she has outburst / this is the walking example of a caged bird / they clipped her wings / and I think of that spotlight and Nina / and at the end / her fight meant nothing / we have new forms of Jim Crow called the prison industrial complex / Black girls can't even identify the magic in them cause the culture of hip hop got them believing you will never be anything more than an accessory / or the only way u can compete behind the mic / is to show your whole ass / be judged on your figure not / your talent / it's like they are walking through pitch black tunnels with broken glass / protruding from the walls and floors / they are seeking our bodies without the minds / and I think of Nina

Simone / 10 fingers / making 88 keys do the unimaginable / She extends / holy water couldn't break this spell / eyes wide open / lips hiding secrets / the kind of secrets that stay behind closed doors / it's France / lips swollen from being slapped in the mouth / lipstick trying to cover / girl / spotlight / and Nina is a Cover Girl / she is gorgeous / but nobody ever told her / they just said you are black / and black girls aren't enough / even when the rainbow shines / and I think of a little girl named Nina / like that student / and my heart can't catch up to all the pain / racing inside me / I find myself lost in the self-hurt thoughts / and then I think of Nina Simone and how her dear sweet friend Betty Shabazz was murdered in her own home by her grandson / named Malcolm / Betty killed by the grandson of her beloved husband Malcolm / And how Nina couldn't love her daughter through her own pain / how that baby girl missed her chance to break the circle of violence in that family / I wonder / would Nina have done it differently / would she have still chosen to fight for us / I see us side-eye cutting each other / and I do so love Black women / we are… / but I'm tired / I have arthritis from gripping my right fist in a Black power stance / see I can't fight anymore / and I want Assata Shakur to come home and love on us / I want to wake up every morning to Angela Davis's smile / cause that smile / can make your heart melt / I want Nikki Giovanni to hold poetry readings in my living room / co-hosted by Sonia Sanchez / I want Laurie Carlos on speed dial / I want her laugh / her wisdom / her joy / her questions / her ability to find the truth through my bullshit / I want Sharon Bridgforth to do my readings hourly / and read me bull-jean stories to help me fall asleep/ I want to take nature walks with Bell Hooks / and when I'm scared have the ability to fall into Harriet Tubman's arms / I want Obama back in the White House / ummmmm… Michelle / not Barack / cause then / and only then / would I truly be safe / but today / right at this moment / I'm tired / I can't carry the weight / so / this is my suicide note / found in the back pocket of my favorite jeans / And I'm not going to apologize / if this makes you feel uncomfortable / But / at the risk of my own sanity / I'm just…

...so/tired

/

I'm just so/

tired

/

I'm just so/

tired /

I'm just so/tired so/so/so/tired

…………….

tir

….

ed

Zell Miller III

Observation

do U / without thinking about it

do U watch the news / and when you see something horrible

a murder / or a robbery / and do you

I don't know / first say a prayer for the victims

cause you are not heartless or free of empathy

but then

right after that

do U

sit there and pray

that the person who committed the crime

they are not / U know

ummmm

pray / like really pray / they are not

U know

Black?

the perpetrator / I mean / do you sit there / and whisper to yourself so no one

hears you / cause you are not a bad person / but

ummmm

and you whisper

"please don't let them be Black / please don't let them be Black"

and then

they show the photo / or say
the name

and you realize / when it's not anybody Black

do you kinda rejoice? / just a little? / give yourself a mental high five?

do you / ever do that? / well / I guess I'm not alone

I mean / I'm just / youknow / I'm just / youknow / saying

just saying / now carry on

Under the Blue Light and Breath
for Laurie Carlos

I see you / overordering in cafes

deciphering dreams / grinning through wasted wisdom

walking away from your buggy / down here we call them carts / but okay

we R

in the center of the city / in Central Market / walking away from your buggy with your purse exposed / selecting organic meat / and you laughing / when I question just how organic is it / U Ma / smelling of sandalwood and freedom your gentle puffy hands / hemp clothing / dancing eyes obliterating malignant misogyny / dancing eyes go right to the point

U R

getting off the train / whimsical / and the light making home /

in your smile / U / seeing my daughter's eyes for the first time

in person / kissing my son on the forehead / after you ask his permission

and sliding your fingertips through my fade / laughing at me

and my / daddy haircut

we R

in a blizzard in St. Paul, Minnesota

me / waking in the Paris suite / your extra bedroom /

me /drowning in boxes / full of historical archives /

the original costumes from *For Colored Girls* /

photos / so many photos / histories in boxes / no labels / legends /

Black theater / cobble stoned history / all right here in a box / photos

so many photos / there is one of you / and a very young Denzel

he is looking at U / with the reverence / of student to master /

I know that look well / photos / so many photos / pictures of

Sam and Tonya's wedding / scripts marked /

and unmarked / yellow at the edges / speaking in loud whispers

to be read / scripts / bouncing with life / and we had music / and words / and stories / and histories / and we had poetry as a binding agent / I miss U / Laurie Carlos / I am in my living room on the outskirts of Austin, Tx

U R

hopping off the train / walking upstairs out of the subway

in Harlem / U tell me the signal may drop / but it stays strong

and you casually say / *"Amiri, I can't hear what you're talking about*

I'm on the phone with my baby, my son" / Then you say to me /

"Amiri, this nigga / wants to read me a poem" / and I swallow my soul

and try to catch the moment / *"wait, did you say ummmm… Amiri? like*

LeRoi Jones Amiri Baraka?" and you laugh your laugh / the laugh of certainty / the laugh of knowledge / and laugh of wisdom / the laugh of comfortable spaces / U now gathered / I can hear your smile through the phone / and U say / *"oh, don't call him that, he's in an intellectual and shit now"* You hand him the phone / and he says *"this is Amiri, who this?"* / and all my fanboy stutters up / and on this day / today / I am reminded that meetings like this / with you / were a regular Tuesday /stories like this dominate my mind / I'm missing you with intense clarity/ and I love you / more than Prince's solo on *Bambi* / and I now understand / subtle blues / I still don't like opera / I do eat more salad with less dressing / I now love Indian food / you would be proud / and pad Thai noodles with chicken / still won't touch calamari / but I did /

finally discover Archie Shepp / and Héctor Lavoe / and I know I'm still 5 references behind / but you love me anyway

Happy b day, Ma

Happy birthday to you, Laurie Smith Carlos

Please know you R missed and / cherished and / praised

daily

from your son / your mentee / and 4ever-friend.

Zell Miller III

In the Shadow of Baldwin

Step studying styling / back 2 the boneyard

Laurie Carlos says / another landfill fills

Masked men / with chicken hearts/ they load their A to the R to the 15eens

and kill at will / and no red state politicians / r willing to stand up

and scream / STOP! / like those innocent victims

I wonder about those babies in Uvalde / had they not been born under Latinx

would those cops have went in

Fuck Greg Abbott!

I'm sick of this wheelchair rocking regime

his lieutenant governor / and attorney general / are criminals

and cowards / shotgun riding in the anti-woman machine

riding winds of the disenfranchised / the boot gets the better again

when u r so used 2 losing / at this game / it gets dull

Like the stinging pain / of knowing / u don't belong

Isolated and unsure / proactive in my step

we move with angular athletic ability

we practice the art of wordplay / In a cocoon

of multi-colored graffiti walls/ we catch breaks / like

Grandmaster Flash

we speak / with sensible authority

and I / star climber / I park my timeship / at 90-degree angle

so I can decree / I'm the one-the one-the one-of me/ and I'm hot

I flame-on / I burn mics 2 a 3rd degree / I leave them disfigured

like a Picasso painting / I swirl / coagulate patterns in perfected principals

unlike the pleasure Janet Jackson didn't get

when Timberlake / exposed her body to the world

and they all screamed / FEAR OF A BLACK BODY / FEAR OF A BLACK BODY

forgetting / they covet it / culture appropriation in mass amounts

I'm like these teens / screaming at their parents / WHAT DAD!

kid / I'm officially over u / so let's move / in sections and spirits

like the Indigenous tribes of texas / who were told get out

by the 2nd President of texas / a man who still has his name on a street sign / that goes

from the north / to the south in this city / lamar /mirabeau buonaparte lamar

he didn't want any Indigenous tribes in his country / so he told them to bounce / but he took their horses / had them walking / and when he felt like

they weren't moving fast enough / good ol boy lamar / he gave orders

2 have them killed / men / women / children /

he had them killed / men / women / and children / genocide

while they sang

We built this city

they built this city on white supremacy

Built this city

They built this city on white supermaccccyyy

and the bell tolls / but for who / star-spangled and mangled / u can't see me

I am the writer / rewritten / in step with the revolution

but I'm taking small strides / like putting my children in charter schools

beeline the moment

don't let their media fool u / dig / if there is a shootout with cops /

and the shooter is white / it's a pretty good chance / that shooter may make it home tonight

or at least get a meal / dylann roof /

or / if that white shooter kills somebody / and cries in court he will walk free /

right kyle rittenhouse / or / if the white killer cries in court / then the black judge will come down and hug them/ right amber guyger / but what do I know

I'm just the writer rewritten like

ancient ceremonies

De La my Soul /

I keep my hands / clutching conscious hip-hop

cause the Stakes R High / there are Potholes in my Lawn /

and it's just Me Myself and I / and I am I b / I am I b / I am I b I am b

I b a yellow brick project / where the sun is too scared to sit

I am standing in kung fu formation

formulating your downfall

Step studying styling / back 2 the boneyard

and we do this in the name of

Vernell Miller / in the name of Brian Keith DeShay

In the name of Laurie Carlos / we do this / in the name of Malcolm X

In the name of Ida B. Wells / in the name of Nikki Giovanni /

in the name of Frida Kahlo / in the name of James Baldwin

In the name of LeRoi Jones and Amiri Baraka

in the name of Akua Njeri / in the name of Fred Hampton Sr, and Jr

we do this / in the name of all the Brown Berets

and the Black Panthers / and all the freedom fighters / pushing through the struggle

we do this in the name of

In the name of

In the name of

step studying styling

I'm through with it!

Zell Miller III

Son Shine Before Sun Shown
for Zell IV my main man 50 grand

Son………..my…….AUTISM!?......My…..son…..

Autism!?

Son

My…….. has……………My…..son…..

autistic

my?

My son has a form of autism

and it keeps changing / on how they want you to say that

First / they said / he has slight… ummm…. slight autism

then it was he has a mild form of Asperger's

2 now / he registers on the autism spectrum

which / is a mouthful / right?

he is fully functional / they say / meaning / I never really understand that term

but he does have problems speaking to strangers / and making eye contact

he forgets things sometimes

but I don't know if that's his autism

or a 16-year-old male / and a slow developing frontal lobe

he is going to have challenges in his life

it's not enough to be a Black male in this country

In a country that has clearly placed so little value on his life

so little value

that a neighborhood watch officiate

idiot was told by police not 2 follow a Black male in Florida

and this officiate / idiot / ignores the warning / follows / and kills a Black male

then walks out of court / found innocent by a jury of his peers

then tweets about / how easy it was to murder a black male

who could just easily be my son… who has…

and get away with it / cause Lives / Black / have never really Mattered

in America / not really

it's not enough that cops can kill you

leave you dying in Cleveland snow

not call for emergency services

Zell Miller III

then when your 14 year old sister comes running / to help you

she is arrested / if that's not enough

you / my son / you / have

autism

defined as a serious developmental disorder

that impairs your ability to communicate

and it took your father / me / years to put the words together in my brain

but they still never came out of my mouth

as if saying it

assured it was fact / your neurodivergent condition

was somehow / a reflection on me

that my past transgressions / have somehow marred you

U know / the sins of the father / as Christians say

but that can't be true / cause white people / who commit horrible crimes against us

their kids go on / collecting the wealth / they created

by rape / murder / stealing / lying / look at the royal family still looting

Haiti / so that can't be true / is the Good Book and the sins only meant for us with

skin-dipped existence

but I still couldn't say the words

not all together /

or maybe if I never spoke it

it would never be true

if I didn't acknowledge the tics

the pacing

the involuntary noises

the rocking

your need to touch textures of things

how loud noises can disturb you

when you go away / in your head where does he go

what wonderful world is he playing in

his speech

maybe if I just did acting exercises / to help his tongue

wrap around the words / like I wrapped him in my arms

If I had just held him longer as a child

Or / maybe I could buy it away

Purchase him the most expensive things / it would be pleased

the autism / it would see this one Black boy is loved

and it would leave

When he stumbled with reading

I could just catch him

Zell Miller III

maybe

It would just disappear

My

Son

Autism

Autistic

Son

My

Like it was somebody's fault / it had to B, right?

Maybe his mother didn't eat the right things while she carried him

Did I not give her enough support / did I not play enough Mozart

and too much Coltrane / while he was growing inside her

did I not talk to him enough while he was in the womb

did I read too much Baldwin and not enough Shakespeare

Was it when she got the flu / when she was 8 months

Son

Autistic

My

And one day as we walked through a store

And he was touching and stroking everything

Feeling their textures

I watched him

Reached out to touch his shoulder

He turned / looking every bit like his mother

Smiling like me

And I just held him

And I said

My son

My son, who happens to have autism

And I love everything about him

And he is perfection personified

son

yes, he is mine

My son

My …… son …… is loved and will always be accepted

by me and we will fight the demons together and no matter what happens

I will scream to the world

that

U R

mine

my son

Zell Miller III

U R

loved

son

Zell Miller III

Light Workers
for Melissa Villarreal

We R the singers of the daybreak

We fold fallen falsehoods into

Tempered tantalizing tasks

Born

Full Moon in our breaths

We bend / not break

Name us

We B

Light workers / warming / in singular solutions

Home

We have sacred solutions / spinning in straight lines / no squares

We keep it simple / such as

Treat as you want to B treated / respect all

When given the opportunity

Choose mercy

We move in silence / and make matter mind / 2 our will

We that example / exhumed / exhausted / but we don't complain

We keep pushing for the greater of us all

This is not for the faint of heart / our wings get heavy / and arms B sore

But we carry on / quiet in our approach

We R cascading waterfalls of hope

When you fall / when you feel you can't take another step / or when your breath

B broken / we B the thoughts / to circumvent the inevitable

We do the impossible / we R the hope

we ancient / and everlasting

Standing / so you can sit

Laughing through

because / we B / the connected cadence

Born with brilliance

We move with quick slow strides

Pace is the moderator / we R the cut creators

The backbeat / the folk song / the story handed down

The legacy you sing / but you can't quite remember / when / or how you learned that melody

that rhythm / we nation born / bright and beautiful / bold

as the axis / in step with truth / separating you from your failure to launch

We dance in the shadows / we stand in the quarter notes / we R the forgiven

We R / the never given up / the harmony / the bassline / the bass drum go

BOOM

We R the children of the sacrifice / the reason you couldn't

Sleep till you told them all / just how much you love them

We R the community minded / blinded by truth / we the I and the Us

The children of the original indigenous nations / on this soil / the daughters of the dust / children of the Aztec / children of the Nile Valley / and Mayan civilizations

The children of the island people / all these cultures / you tried to erase history

We R / home / yours / and ours / we B / the light / the workers / the brigade

We B the ingenuity / created in the quiet spaces / we b the progress of a fist folded

We b the promise of the now / we b the free legal aid / the free afterschool program / the community liaisons / the nurses / the youthcare workers / the artists of all discipline / the volunteers / the first to arrive / the last to leave / the organizers

the fighters for U / the listener / in a pandemic / we R the construction workers

the delivery drivers / the janitors / the stockers / the cashiers / the bakers /

the sanitation workers / the bus drivers / the teacher going in /

even

when her own children / R virtual schooling / we R the witnesses /

the assistants / the mothers / and the / all of us / we R the singers of the daybreak

we fold fallen falsehoods into / tempered / tantalizing tasks / born

Full Moon in our breaths

We bend / not break

Name us

We B

Light workers / warming / in singular solutions

We R

The seekers

the home again

and again

and again

Zell Miller III

4 Those Who Were Not Protected, But Served

I can't breathe

let's examine nature / let's examine choice

let's examine the will of man / as it's told through an ancestral voice

or the scripture / did I mention / and while we on that shit

let's examine mythology / and the twisted tales / of europeans a bit

now dig / is it he who holds the weapon / to make everybody bow down / is it he

who controls the narrative / and how it all went down / but let me pause a sec

take my breath and shit / let it marinate a bit / as I examine

my use of pronouns / and shit / see / I just used my penis privilege / instead of saying them / or she / I could have chosen they / I said he / looks like / I / 2 / am caught up / in the western / white man lies / and the oppressive games / they play but / let's get it back to stories / like the glory / of the immaculate conception

that story was stolen / from the African lands / real fact / let's examine

the real story / of the so-called / son of man / and what if that power that we pray 2 / was actually Black / that would explain a lot / like / Y white men and women / kill / maim / rape / and lie / to get that number one spot / let's talk about

the power of perception / the power of suggestion / like / if I repeat something enuf U / R bound to believe the revelations /

4 example / like what if U heard

nigga / U ain't shit / nigga / your momma ain't shit / nigga / your daddy ain't shit / nigga / your brother ain't shit / nigga / your sister ain't shit / nigga / your partner ain't shit / shit / nigga / U are worthless / and U hold no value / and shit / now let me look in this mirror / just to make things / a little bit clearer / while I'm pointing out / I know they pointing back / but / let's get it back 2 facts / like the

Tuskegee experiment / is fact / inject a bunch of Black farmers / with syphilis

and don't tell them / in fact / send them home to spread that disease /

to their wives and kids / but / the united snakes / still / ain't coming up

off that / 40 acres and a mule / Black / now let me pause a bit / close my eyes and shit / so I can see / they gave some of those indigenous tribes / casinos

while descendants of slaves got jim crows / I'm with sista Nina / I'm on some mississippi godamn / but texas ain't no better / even up north / where jackets are required for the winter there are places / I can't enter

and it's not commonplace / in the city of lakes / a Black face in need / tells the officer with his knee on his neck

"YO! I can't breathe"

lungs weakening / while George Floyd pleads / and later in courts / cameras show officers

Zell Miller III

who lie / like their orange-colored commander and chief / imagine / your son

tells U / he is going jogging / as he usual does / but Arbery is hunted / and then eliminated by racists thugs / terroristic acts by domestic terror actors

white men / father and son / tag-teamed

yeah / Martin had a dream / but Malcolm had an M1/ how do we continue to

co-exist in society / that's so Hellbent on our destruction / where are

my P.T.S.D. prescriptions / and it all gets to be 2 much / sometimes

but we can't rewind time / and my chest feels like an avalanche is present

and I

can't

catch

my

breath

air escapes from lungs

and

I can't

I

ca n't

b r e a t h e

Zell Miller III

Quiet Spaces

It's in the quiet spaces / where the traces of love / are the sweetest residue

Candy-sweet / like weekly allowance on a Friday afternoon / it's 1976

and there I am / rubbing / two quarters together

that 50 cent is burning a hole in my pocket

the sound of the ice cream man / bouncing down your block

the Texas sun / on a July afternoon / singes your skin

why does the line / seem / to never move / when you are in it

then it happens

your turn

you get that / red / white and blue / firecracker rocket / and it's multicolored

sugary sweetness / dances down your throat / and it drips down your arm

sending sweet salutations to your soul

that's what you remember / in the quiet spaces

like your son / tasting sweet potatoes / for the first time

7 months old licking / his lips / and the energy / running through

his entire body pining for more / like it's his last meal

Or the grapefruit-sized eyes of your daughter

on her first birthday

when she pressed her entire hand into her birthday cake

and you and her / were the only 2 people / who found it funny

It's in the quiet spaces

of 2:59 a.m.

slight hum of the ceiling fan

mind racing

remembering / with pinpoint accuracy

first time you held them

both

first human touch

was me

both times

senses now flooded

their smell

the never again softness of their skin

against your fingertips

images rush

fighting for placement

lining up to get pole position

first bike rides

Zell Miller III

first bottles

first fevers

laying with them till they fall asleep

Christmas mornings

Or them / laying in your bed

singing

"*itsy bitsy spider*"

and after an evening of homework help

fighting over TV time

proper etiquette at the table

chew with your mouth closed, dawg

We don't sing at the table baby / yes / you have to eat the veggies love

put the dog down, Blaise

no, Zell / you can't have another dessert

no, Blaise / you can't play Minecraft anymore tonight

it's a school night

Zell / being on your phone / is the same as being on the computer, dawg

and it's after 8 p.m. / time to shut it down

Kids / do you have your clothes ready for tomorrow?

Did you wash your face?

Did you brush your teeth?

And after all that

it's in these quiet spaces

you remember those captured images

and moments of them sitting in your bed singing

"*The itsy bitsy spider crawled up the water spout…*"

and you realize / there is nowhere else / you would rather b.

Zell Miller III

My Hero Slept in the Same Room as Me

thank U

4 teaching me the precision of a behind-the-back pass

more than that / U taught me how 2 dream / how 2 imagine / how 2 pretend

thank U

for showing me / through your actions / creativity

can be more than a verb / when I was sick with asthma

you brought breath back 2 me / with paper action figures / U created 4 me

still don't know how you could stomach shredded wheat / or Spider-Man

"Brother" doesn't do justice / and it's too weak a word / U taught me true artistic discipline / by your determination / 2 journal / 2 dream past the limits of Springdale Gardens / and Dallum Drive / I see you flying past on your gold BMX bike / seeing the world in 3D / discipline of an artist / how U taught yourself

how 2 play guitar / by replaying Jimi Hendrix / videos over / and over / U stepped in when Daddy or Keith could not / when momma told me no to the white Pumas in 8th grade / it was U / who walked in the gym / right before basketball practice with that shoebox / and U were still in high school / U spent your check on me your generosity / knew no limits when it came 2 me friend is too weak a word / did U know / U saved my life / when U left for Arizona / chasing dreams as dreamers do / No one knew the pain I was carrying / what an actor I am

/ or maybe U did know / because the last thing U said 2 me was / read this book by Nikki Giovanni / later / when I had a .380 pistol in my mouth / I looked down / that book smiled up 2 me / I read the first poem / and put the pistol down / I am an artist because of U / U with the camera around your neck / seeing the world in 3D / I chased you in the artistic space / and fell into acting / then writing / I see us in Austin summers ordering fast food that U paid 4 / communicating without speaking / mentor is too weak a word / our Newbreed band bouncing along / I am because U did a Black child / outcasted by family / It never stopped U / from being gracious / or dreaming / I started writing because I watched U

love is too weak a word

I hope thank U is enough

I am the father I am / the husband I am / the artist I am / because U / Tony / U showed me through actions

so

thank U

Big bro / for Hendrix / and Sly / and the musical history/ how to approach a girl / with honesty

thank U

for seeing me through the fits / and tantrums / temper

Zell Miller III

thank U

for making me / who Ashley loves / who Zell IV admires / and who Marley aspires 2 B / and the precision of a behind-the-back pass

never disappoints peace and blessings 2 U / big bro almighty

Zell Miller III

Bang!

since the first click / of the first shackle / to the first African

bAng!

since the first slap / from the first whip / to the first back / of the first African

baNg!

who was first shackled / beaten / humiliated / abused / sold / murdered

banG!

Lynching is an american tradition

Date Line: May 19, 1918 Mary Turner / LYNCHED

4 speaking about her innocent husband / who was lynched days before

Mary Turner / pregnant / was beaten / hung / and her unborn child

was cut from her body

and S T O M P E D to death

by the crowd of over 60 white men

bang!

Lynching is an american tradition

Date Line: June 15, 1930 / Dennis Hubert was arrested for quote

"being disrespectful to a white woman"

he was dragged from jail by 40 plus white men / beaten / then murdered

his crime / he said / "somebody better get that drunk woman home"

a white woman / fell in the street / in the center of town

later / it was proved / she was drunk

B A N G!

tradition in america is lynching / in america / lynching is tradition / Bang!

it was custom for Black men / and women to be jailed / dragged from jail by mobs

usually / white hooded figures / creeping through the night / armed with fire power

ropes / fist / beat bodies bloody / pull triggers

BANG!

hang bodies from innocent Elm trees / make a night of it / bring families / eat food / laugh / show their children / take photos / get into fist fights over the severed penis

of swinging bodies for keepsakes / place the trophy on their mantels

brag to neighbors / make postcards to send to families around the country

it got so bad / the postmaster general / of america / had to make it illegal

4 the postcards / to be mailed / the postcards of charred Black flesh

swinging from trees

bang!

since the first recorded lynching in 1882 / 2 the last recorded lynching in 1968

on record there are

3,446 / 3,446 / 3,446

Black Men / Black Women / Black Children

LYNCHED

from the deep south / to the pacific northwest

BANG!

there is a history of murdering Black children / in this country

there is a history of people / in law enforcement / working hand in hand

with courts / and juries / witness tampering / crucial evidence goes missing

local and federal law enforcement administrations

bringing their own brand of justice / or rather / injustices / to people who look like us

and those who are guilty / serve no time / and get celebrated in their community

so / it should be no surprise / when a Black child is murdered / those responsible / if they have white complexion / receive no punishment for their crime

many in the white community will say / *but what does this have to do with us*

many in the white community will say / *racism is something of the past / right?*

but the community will say

Date Line: August 28, 1955 / Emmett Till / a 14-year-old Black boy / guilty

for having the audacity / to speak to a white woman / or whistle at a white woman

Emmett Till / a Chicago kid / who didn't know the landscape of the deep south

for that / he was beaten / shot / his barely breathing body was then /

tied to a 70-pound fan / tossed into the Tallahatchie River

even the river could not let such a brutal crime go unnoticed / his beaten body barely recognizable by his own mother / who made sure he had an open casket so america / could see the brutality done to Black bodies

there is a history of young Black men being accused / found guilty with no crime

just somebody's word / then the mob comes out / those young men / murdered

Bang!

Date Line: September 15, 1963 / Birmingham, Alabama

Addie Mae Collins / Cynthia Wesley / Carole Robertson / Carol Denise McNair

4 little Black girls

who sat innocently / in the basement of the 16th Street Baptist Church

preparing for the weekly sermon / while 2 members of the Ku Klux Klan

planted dynamite / under the basement floor

B A N G!!!!!!!!!!!!!!

not one day of jail time was served by their killers / they later laughed about in a magazine article / and confessed to the murders

bang!

since the original constitution of america said / Black people are 3/5 of a human

Black life in America has no value / we are property

Bang!

Date Line: March 16, 1991 / Compton, Ca / Latasha Harlins a 15-year-old Black girl

accused of stealing a bottle of juice / video shows the store owner / grabbing Latasha / and Latasha fighting back / then / she is shot in the back

as she tries to leave / the store owner received no jail time / for killing a Black girl

the same time this case was prosecuted / a man accused of animal cruelty

received 30 days in jail / but the life of a Black child / only 5-years probation

we are asking / like you / Marvin / "what's going on" / Bang!

but America is about that equality / that is what you want me to believe

that Black bodies have value and worth / right?

but there is a Fruitvale Station / please don't make us Fruitvale station

shame on you / San Francisco / shame on you / San Francisco

Tatiana / your father didn't have 2 die that way / Oscar Grant III / they do it here / too

Bang! / Byron Carter, Jr. / Bang! / Sophia King / Bang! / Kevin Brown / Bang! / Nathaniel Sanders / Bang! / Bang!

All in Austin / all dead /all Black

BANG!

Dear white America

telegram for you

Stop

Zell Miller III

Racism still exists

Stop

Black and brown parents watch their children walk out of the house / and there is a reality that is the last time they may see them

Stop

We are tired of cops

district attorneys / judges / and juries of their peers / not ours / releasing them from punishment

Stop

Our hands are up

Stop

Our hands are up we are not resisting

Stop

Our hoodies are down

Stop

U can stop this tradition

Stop

U can break the cycle

Stop

Parents shouldn't outlive their children

Stop / fathers should make it home

Stop

Eric Garner should have made it home

Stop

Trayvon Martin / we will never forget U

Stop

may zimmerman be haunted

by your essence until the day he dies

Stop

Michael Brown

you will not die in vain / we promise

Stop!

Stop!

Stop!

Officer / please!!!!!

BANG!!!

Zell Miller III

Zell Miller, Jr. a.k.a. Daddy
(from the play "*Oh...Sh*t...It's a Girl!*")

there is something to be said / at 71 / his suits fit him well

still has a full head of hair / still does sit-ups / and push-ups

daily

still gets out in that truck of his / and grinds

daily

still collecting scrap steel / or loading up lawnmowers / to manicure lawns

hustle hard / that's my daddy / his smile still engages

and his eyes still twinkle at the sight of his children / and grandchildren

somehow / his pockets stay deep for his kids / but his love is a bottomless ocean

and I want my children to speak of me / with the reverence we do for him

there is something to be said / at 71 / 9th grade education

unfulfilled personal dreams / he has not missed a performance

since I started in 7th grade / he is there / legs crossed

program in his right hand / and until he can't / I know he will B there

and / as a child / I didn't always understand his cryptic advice

and / as a child / I was sometimes embarrassed / when he came to pick me up rolling up to my school / in his dump truck / or roaming the halls

looking for me in his work clothes / sweaty back / dirty boots

the symbols of a hard day's work / not knowing then / that was his sacrifice

so we could live / with two who depend on me / now / I get it

there is nothing you wouldn't do / so your children can have

there is something to be said / at 71 / he comes to birthday parties

even when it's just the three of us / and he gives the oldest

lunch money for the month / even when he's been told / it's already been paid

and his hugs are easy to fall into / and he can't understand the video game

his grandson with his name is so excited about / and trying to explain to him

or what exactly his granddaughter is trying to tell him

about Princess Tiana and her pot / and how she is now a frog

but he is present / he is laughing / and he is loving

and on those mornings / when I wake alone in a quiet house

sitting in front of my computer / with my hands curved to create

but everything the muse just woke me with / is now gone

the screen is blank / I sit frozen / the voices come first low / then spark into a full out press *"you can't do it / you never could do it / you're a joke / give up*

go watch TV / leave this creativity shit alone /

it ain't ever going to happen / man / so just stop"/ I think of him

Daddy

sitting there with his grandchildren / smiling / present / at 71

I smile / and think / there is something to be said / and I will say it

then the pen sparks / fingers move / words pirouette across the page

because / he and I / are worth it

Zell Miller III

Jimi Was a B-Boy

his hand clasps around her neck / she moans / his hand squeezing

she shrieks at the shrouded shrine / then releases

she maneuvers / moist manipulated manic moans

working under his fingering frets / he uses the sciences of dirt / cause dirt holds

the DNA of God / you touch any part of Earth / Mother Ground

palm flat / and it will leave a mark / but he don't fret

he just works frets / on his Stratocaster / turned upside on the down / breath brings beats between the 2 and 4 / and Jimi's left hand / is guided by the prettiest angel

youknow that X-saint / sitting slyly seducing sinful saturated sounds / while Gabriel waits on high alert / he's tuning triumphant trumpets in d-minor / his threat level is changing like leaves in the Carolinas / it's turning orange / it's turning brown

it's turning yellow / it's turning

"WAAHHHH-dowww WAH-nuh-wah-nee-NEE BRAAWWWWHH-bwow-bwow-nyaaaa-nyaah REE-nee-nee-WAHHHH! Neeeee-WEE-dah-WEE!"

it's a psychedelic dust magic that runs back through a cord / that is connected to an amp / and inside the amp / are tubes / they are exploding / imploding and the soundman / is about to have a nervous breakdown / but that Afro Alien

he pulls it all back / and plays it / loose / and cool / and God dammit / he's cool

he's cool / like a perfect performed windmill by crazy legs / and he's got visions

of clouds / he remembers the sounds of free falling / X-paratrooper

imagine that irony / he jumped from planes / like he jumped from heaven

and now / he takes that tidal wave of sound and he rides it / like a skilled surfer before long he is commander and / chief / he throws a nod to the soundman

and he tells him

"ummm.. there's no beef, baby, youknow / it's all groove"

and / at that moment / he became we / and we he

so it's 1984 / and we are standing / with our arms folded feet spread apart

head tilted / now / is it a coincidence at that time / we rock parachute pants

like Jimi was an X-paratrooper / and I remember the first time / somebody told me Herbie Hancock was a jazz musician / I laughed in their face / how the fuck a jazz musician / gonna make / a joint like / "Rockit" for the breakers to break 2 / and my uprock was sweet / I remember the first time / I saw *Breakin'* / 1984

Northcross Mall movie theater / and black ass Robert Easley / sat next to me

and he literally / jumped out his seat and rolled down the aisles / cause he had just seen Jesus and Jesus was a Black man named Turbo / Robert

caught the holy ghost / like those old ladies / on Sunday morning

on cue / after Reverend Frankly / wiped / his dry forehead / a 3rd time

with that white hankie / see B-boys / been trying to / B / and ain't that the question

I mean / even old thieving-ass Shakespeare / knew the answer to that

see / B-boys / been trying to B / long before / 41 shots shots shots shots

shots shots shots shots shots / Amadou Diallo/ shots shots shots shots shots shots / it's just my wallet / shots shots shots shots / Breonna Taylor / shots shots shots shots shots shots shots / Nathaniel Sanders Jr /shots shots shots shots shots shots / Trayvon Martin / shots shots shots shots shots shots shots / Michael Ramos

shots shots 41 shots like / Sophia King

long before whips / long before chains / long before

boats took trips across the ocean with human cargo / B-boys

been trying 2 B / better / and in our attempts to B better / we can't forget our past

we have to take that back feed / and feedback our hungry spirits

and create new songs / cause Jimi knew / a B-boy's bluez

it ain't always sad / and I'm sorry / not sorry white America

fuck a rock star / U can't have him / like u can't have Tina Turner

or Sly Stone / no / they belong to us

see

James

Marshall

Hendrix

was a

B-boy

B-boy

who happened to play

"the bluez baby / youknow"

Momma Moon
for Vernell Miller

(from the play *Ballot Eats the Bullet*)

Standing / leaning against the entryway / she sway to the beat only she can hear / cigarette smoke dancing from her right hand / there she be / Pepsi in her left hand / no liquor just her reality be the catalyst / she brown / be Black / Black like two sugars / and two creams / that's how she takes her coffee / prefers her skin to be pitch night black / but she caramel / either way she flawless / she beautiful/ like that aisle in the grocery store where our hair products don't be / no / we the aisle over / urban / but that's a developer's term / but she say we elegant / exquisite / she beautiful and her natural color collides with a western reality / unlike every other Black family in our housing project / there is no picture of Jesus / or Martin Luther King / ask her why / she says / *"I ain't putting no white man on my wall / and I don't want them in my house"* / and as for Martin Luther King / she say / *"he an asshole / he had those kids marching / getting arrested / putting them in harm's way"* / she say *"I like Malcolm X / he was a handsome-ass Black man"* she say / *"Malcolm X was fine"* / and I ain't never again / heard nobody say / Malcom X / was fine / she makes me laugh / my Mother Moon / got a tattoo / on her right ankle of a black rose she says it's symbolic / she symbiotic / one with water / earth / and air / swings her words from the hip / where she carried me / structured / Goddess / be a Black woman / all praises due / she holds the universe / then spin night to the day while tempting waves to crash / and Earth to part and catch every tear with a taste of salt / multi-tasking be a Black woman's regular / she regular / regular genius / she B / Mother / my Mother Moon / cigarette hanging loose from the right corner of her African-kissed lips / right hand on the frying pan / chicken popping in yesterday's grease corn bread browning in the oven / green beans bubbling in bacon / eyes disciplining without her ever having to get up from her seat / she raise that left eyebrow / that's when you know you going to get it / left hand making Afro puffs for me / phone nestled between her jawbone and shoulder she speaking in her white woman voice / over enunciating and over articulating / handling the bill collector with kid gloves / as she tugs gently at my Afro puffs / wrapped in rubber bands / and a rainbow of barrettes / how she does this with one hand / is beyond me / but my Mother Moon / hangs up the phone / and proceeds to speak in three different tones / like a full choir / so / all her children get their instructions / and that chicken don't burn / and the cornbread is perfect / with no timer / and we all eat / and she sips her coffee / calculating her next move / she told me / *"girl / know / you are somebody's dream / an ancestor sat down / and dreamed of this very moment for you / so don't let them down / don't ever accept failure / cry when you need to / then get up / and get it done"* / that's my Momma Moon / who walked out of this existence / and found her way to that garden in Heaven / to sit with our ancestors / she took her journey / July 30th 2015 / and when the world comes at me in waves / and I think I can't swim / I remember the sound of my Momma Moon's voice / and I make a cup of coffee / I put it next to her ashes / and in the quiet / I just sit / prepare / focus / then I go conquer / just like / my Momma Moon / who is always / sitting right at the center of my heart / questioning my choices / and pushing me to do right / be kind / and whole / I miss U / with every fiber of my being / till we meet again

and the chicken / don't burn / Ma

When Is Freedom No Longer Free?
for Banned Book Week 2025

when is freedom / no longer free

when I fall between the pages of books

I have yet to be assaulted / by ideas / truths / or different perspectives

I love reading / I love escaping inside the portals the pages provide

4 me to fall into and out of / these worlds known and unknown

These pages provide history or context / and I love the touch of a book in my hand

I love the white pages / highlighted by the black words

I love how the words / the ideas / dance across / and through my mind

as a parent / believe me / I understand the categories / and levels of subject matters

I understand guardrails are necessary / for some concepts

I understand every household / has a right to decide

what / and how / hard or controversial subjects should be handled

under their roof

what I don't understand

as I stand on so called free soil

how a small group / can make decisions / for me and my household

when is freedom / no longer free / so / I will exercise my freedom

To speak up and speak out

I dedicate this / 2 the writers

who braved their own trauma 2 give others an access point

2 help them through / similar situations / or maybe 2 bring attention

2 a subject that sometimes / we feel is too big / and the writer says

here is a reference point / 2 jump-start the conversation

this is 4 the tellers of their own truth / who are punished / posthumously

this is 4 the curious minds / that seek knowledge / and understanding

this is 4 the bookshelves that now lay bare

this is 4 the false sense of freedom that covers us / forged in the dirt of this land / then the tents fold when a brisk breeze / hints of a subject matter that challenges the norm

this is 4 the young readers / who can't wait 2 age up / so they can read that one book

Zell Miller III

and that one book

is now gone

this is 4 the parents / who stand on a liberal bridge / but now can't cross it / with their children / because the books are banned

this is 4 my mother / who had her freedom restricted as a youth in the capital city of Texas / and now her grandchildren / have books removed from their libraries

this is 4 the librarians caught in the crossfire of political dribble

4 the librarians who only want 2 help with the injection of literacy / but now are left on an island

floating in a sea of distance / who are now the unwilling / cast as Cerberus

I ask again

when is freedom no longer free

This is 4 Toni Morrison / James Baldwin / *The Perks of Being a Wallflower* / *All Boys Aren't Blue* / *Sold* / *The Hate U Give* / *A Court of Mist and Fury*

4 Sarah J. Maas / George R. R. Martin / Khaled Hosseini

4 any and all / who are shackled for their truths

their stories / their words / their attempt to cross lines /

2 unite us

2 help us see it from a different angle

we will never be united / if we continue

2 allow words / and ideas to keep us separateed

when is freedom / no longer free

as a youth / we usta say

"sticks and stones will break my bones/ but words will never hurt me"

if we continue to stay divided by words / the contusions to our basic rights / will never heal / and united / how can we stand

if we allow words to keep us divided

I ask again

When

Is

Freedom

No

Longer

Free

Zell Miller III

Refugee… Me? 2nd Movement
(from the play *Echo of a Refugee… Me?*)

i am the intersection / the center where two lines cross / or clash

i am the shrinking percentage points of those who have skin like mine

i am the intersection / sewn into the roots a city decaying with

clear identity its roots are dying / this city B a gentrified cavity untreated

this city be a back-room abortion / forced by politrickians / gone bad

this city be the morning after pill / so unaffected to demon seeds

seething / these white squatters / imperialist in their strides

demographic demigods designing destruction / neighborhood / by neighborhood

with little care / and absolutely no regrets / who they trample

i B the new nigga

here to make waves

modern day slaves

get lynched

not by white hooded figures / but by multi-cultural real estate agents

who smile while they

tell you / in a calm voice

it will cost more than a kidney / to live in these new neighborhoods

these so called

new neighborhoods

where I stood as a young figure

shadowed by a streetlight / properties entrenched on the East Side

of the divide / that B I-35 / neighborhoods

where we never saw people who looked like U

Unless / they were wearing police blue

or suits and ties / armed with pamphlets

wanting to speak on Jehovah / and wanting us Black skins to witness / I stand in places

where people who now reside

wouldn't even drive

through / when the Sun went down

I'm MLK and 12th street

a stretch of street

Zell Miller III

where the gun shots compete

with the religious wails of St. James Baptist choir / who preached on the evils of homosexuality

but the choir director was the evil U warned about / and your pastor / if the streets are correct

but let's move on

I am the intersection of your precious SoCo

where before the food trucks were pushed out / I remember that section of downtown

had the highest area of prostitution

See I go back like K.N.O.W.

pre K.A.Z.I. / back when K.N.O.W.

wasn't segregated by genre / where you could hear the Doobie Brothers / Stevie Wonder / Johnny Cash / Kool and the Gang / all on the same playlist

I am staying up till 12 midnight / with fresh blank tapes in the boom box

ready to record the master mix on K.A.Z.I. / I am / the never shopping at the H.E.B on 7th street

cause it was always nasty / this city that embraced Lance Armstrong /

but never took back his key to the city / I am the copious colored skipper pins of AquaFest the gun shots that changed the scope and attendance / at Rosewood Juneteenth

the house party where youth were assaulted by cops

that lead to the so called block-long building / filled with activities for youth

that got shrunk down / to the sad sack of shit called / the Millennium center

I am the neglected pillars / overlooked by new niggas / at the Black Chamber

who are trying to create a history / never was / with people who ain't been here

or from here / but get named Austin's Black Creatives / I am the intersection of sports and race

the torn orange and white / number 20 of Earl Campbell / as he bullied his way to a Heisman

and Daryl K. Royal / keeping the doors closed to Black athletes till 1970

but he gets a stadium named after him / this is the city defined

the pricing out of the darker hue / this domino put in position / by the wile e. weasel will winn

the mayor / with his real estate cohorts / remember when they closed down cruising 6th street

the closing of Catfish Station / the always-strained relationship of A.P.D

Zell Miller III

from another brown or black person shot and killed / with bullets owned by Austin's finest

I am Sofia King's last breath / Daniel Rocha's last blink / toll roads filing for bankruptcy

I am the Black theater artist who can't book the space / supposedly built for people like me

with my friend's name written across the door / the mural on the wall of the Carver Library

I am Booker T. projects / and the 250,000 dollar new barn style housing facing the projects,

let's see how long those projects stand / I am a Sunday drive through Givens Park

the fire hydrant unhinged / shirtless dark-skin bodies smiling under the Texas Heat

I am the intersection of growth / and a live music capital of the world

with a noise ordnance / I am the Stevie Ray statue / and his stolen Hendrix licks

I am Sam's Bar-B-Que on Saturday afternoon / not the fake-ass Franklin's with his salt and pepper seasoning / I am the Victory Grill still standing through the weight of the giant

called GENTRIFICATION / pushing me down

like a bully on the playground

of Sims Elementary / I am my city evolving into something I

can no longer recognize

no longer love / no longer respect / no longer rep

I am the intersection crossed / and left

alone

U Beautiful Flowing U

I.

U river flow 2 a soothing stop / take breath

U river b awake / pushing pass the past

U river flow fluid / flowing functioning / full no longer

U river stopped by patterns to plug the flow

the foliage swimming in u river and around u river

like the eastern redbud adapts shifts like u river accepting that

change is the law of life rooted and standing strong like the live oak the pecan and cedar elm trees give perches and housing to the feathered fellows singing in

harmonic keys there are circles of respect moments of life swimming in and around me the dragon and damsel flies hover in constant motion

shimmering off my reflection they provide for the bats

as the painted sunsets say goodnight

the bats become hunters moving in solitary silence or small uncoordinated groups

nature will nature we don't need pristine perfect plots

U river throughout the world providing for the ecosystems

of all nature's creatures humans included

I b the historically common

denominator where life flowed find me as center my cousins in grand standing like the Nile, the Amazon, the Yellow, the Tigris, the Euphrates, and the powerful Mississippi and our health is a mirror reflection of the world's health

if 40 percent of us are well what does that say about the other 60 percent and all life breathing on this planet we should b living and respecting in a circle of return

U river too often taken for granted that I will just continue to flow nice and smooth

but past times U river has roared like 1869 taking the city under tow and breaking through the 1893 dam rising again in 1900 and 1935

and 1981 U river unapologetic in the flow colonies of humans gathering at and around u throughout their time now u find yourself in the

position of having to adjust to me because your ground water

is fading and aquifers are dissipating and drought goes strong

neglecting that U river provide birds with sustenance they dipped into U

and feed their babies with the many worlds created in U river universe

the feathered friends who are another tier in this ecosystem

systematic sustainability swims here from the insects to the

humans who pull fish from the Montopolis Bridge

to standing chest deep in U river gently waves

U river helped on the road to salvation

U river providing for worlds too small to b seen

Zell Miller III

to the multitudes of feathered friends in relation to your ever
changing flow u river never the same with footprint
or dive of a bird u river constant is change and change
is the law of life because u river don't change u river
transforms and the worlds connected to the flow
shift as well

Zell Miller III

II.

I river u river we river dance

I river u river we river dream

I river u river we river sing

I river u river we river change

chat

we river on 4th of July we river on star-filled nights / we river / we gather

to witness the bats descend on our city / at this critical time of disconnection

we know there is nothing more powerful than the word we / or the phrase we the people we the river / we the birds / we the trees / we the fish / we the river

like we the people / some may parade some may protest some may listen some may shout, but we must all find our common ground and cast singular focus to connect we can no longer b content with the I for we are here now together

"we must be willing to let go of the life we planned so as to have the life that is waiting for us"

and in the we / we must b in lockstep with the river all the creatures

feathered and scaled change is uncomfortable, but here together as we the people

I was told when giving the opportunity u should always choose mercy

our future is closer than before and as a unit we can uplift each other

change the culture move with purpose we got this

we are the change we seek we together can light the path

this is not a mission to save we river

no

this is the beginning of our shift

culture change maybe our lawns won't b as green, but our connection to we river

will b stronger and fresh water will stretch longer we are each a layer of the

ecosystem I don't believe we can't change I'm old enough to remember a time when no one had a cell phone, remember that? we are so amazing in our adaptability we can make sure the lights never dim and shine into the future let's reflect off the mirror that is we river and b the change we seek

inside all of us because only together can we make this happen

I river u river we river dance

I river u river we river dream

I river u river we river sing

I river u river we river lives

Zell Miller III

Pages of Light
for Raasin and crew

the lifeline of a city should not b its skyline

or the landmarks that identify a city

it should not b pie charts or graphs that inform you of its economic power

no, the lifeline of a city is the pipeline of its people

beautiful souls who stand in their whole selves and their diverse conditions

individuals, rather than statistics, establish harmonious ways 2 coexist

in this city by the river, Austin

there is no greater bookmark of equality than a library's door

like the spine of a book

open and allow the community's pages 2 illuminate

the power of connection through story, myth, and spoken history

allow these pages of light 2 b the breadcrumbs that lead you back

2 this space of salutations and community

welcome to these pages of light

Zell Miller III

Discovering Diamonds While Trying 2 Touch a St. Paul Moon

I.

there is no sky like this sky

hazy shade of gray

sunlight is an often / abandoned foster child between homes

and street watching wondering where the next meal will come from

I examine the clap of tires on slushy streets closing eyes to the rush

of snowflakes on my face my feet crush past diamonds in a breath

I remember it's frozen water / bundled packages laugh past me

their feet crush past the diamonds / but with quicker pace

bound up with hoodies removed / and backpacks / and giggles

their floating transportation in high yellow color and black lettering

the lettering is descending / unlike the chill of this real winter moment

hard to digest / for me southern in my balance / and the bundled packages

unintentionally make me question my ego / as they descend off their transport

dingy from the wet frozen weather / but the soundtrack of babies laughing is a pleasant backbeat to my lonely concerto

walking alone / my feet crush past what I perceive 2 B diamonds

but the sight of my own breath / reminds me it's frozen water

the bundled packages / seem content in this normalcy and willingness

to deal with below 0 degrees

they are a sweet resolve / and I no longer need the Sun for support

but still / there is no sky like this sky

II.

therapy is the night

figure the distance from here to there

missing is reserve

the hands of the winter moon are unreachable

shadows glow against the snow / keeping time with the rhyme

booming from my portable cd player

I'm speaking out loud lyrics / and maneuver my tongue 2 drums

and allow electronica 2 transport me

wrapped in layers while calculating the distance / between memory and reality

I try 2 decipher the visions / now laid out in front of me

in the form of my own breath

they make classic shapes against the canvas of winter

so stark in the form of my own breath

they make classic shapes against the canvas of winter

and they are approachable / but withhold their names

I am within the night / shaking resistance songs under my hooded sweatshirt

and the distance between each step / I catch a glimpse of the now

and it hums like Khalil Gibran / at the table he offers me a seat

Laurie Carlos said Khalil was a gentle man

but I can't stop moving in this winter night for fear to be frozen to death

statue like the giant Charlie Brown character throughout this city

my program files remain virus free

I love the night / and the frozen ground reflects me

I've been waiting close 2 to the edge in my own reality / 4 some time now

waiting close 2 the edge of love

trying 2 reach the familiar respiration of your smile

but it stays hidden in this winter rush

and Khalil just laughs / and says / *"keep digging, poet; it will eventually find you"*

Zell Miller III

III.

In this St. Paul, Minnesota adjacency

I move only within a few blocks of my new neighborhood / by choice

I remind myself / this space / these streets / this food / this quiet

is temporary / traveling artist / have script and stage / will travel

the 70s vibe of my played-out orange carpet / gives me a broader context

2 the spirits walking non-connected between the walls / of this one room

provisional / but it's not home / nothing central Texas about this / at all

Lourdes and Annette's haunting melodies coupled

with Sharon's episodical poetry and parables come to pass

are mere side dishes / to Laurie's intricate and soul stirring jazz aesthetic movement / and the use of breath / augmenting the scenes into epic jazz bombs

make for sleepless nights / and long hot baths in the morning

the snow fell from dusk to dawn yesterday / and I haven't seen the Sun

but I'm not cold / and still I keep missing the moment / and I keep 4getting

the moment never leaves / I just chose not 2 see it /

but I am making my new neighborhood expand with old / new

ability

remembering to release / and I am learning / 2 release more

with every waking moment / learning 2 use breath / with action

learning to trust / the unverified / learning 2 trust in my ability

2 trust in my learning / 2 believe only in the universe

learning 2 remember / I am a divine extension of God

and still there is no sky / like this sky

Zell Miller III

IV.

I wake / walk into the dream of U

can I know the tender of your smile

B present in the symphony of your walk

Ashley

U have such a sexy… inhale

please notify the proper authorities

tell them I'm lost 2 your touch

tell them I fell into the mahogany of your eyes and can't find my way back

tell them I feel like I'm writing to deaf ears

tell them I left insurance for you and Zell and Marley

but you knew nothing about that

remind our babies / their father / may be miles and leap years away

but I don't go a second without them on my mind

tell them they are the profitable 4th quarter of my emotional recession

Ashley / my beloved / is it a mistake I partake your face / and you mine

even when I'm so far away / and the technology of touch / is not an option

if so

I will just dream a new

but my love

what will U do?

V.

there is no sky like this sky

gray and ageless

tight and retractable

epic like a Pink Floyd track

innovative like a Prince lyric

before he was married / and had beef with Warner Brothers

reckless like teenage sex

I'm decisive in the judgement of frozen water

never have I seen such beauty in nature

cold water dropping from the sky

0 below and I still sleep with a fan on

I'm looking for my bridge into this reality

the moon looms large and approachable in Austin, Tx

but here in St. Paul, Minnesota it grows beyond touch

and there is no smell in the snow

I approach time carefully

hypnotized by the burning truth of this wind

this sky / dig / I know / I have never seen a sky like this before

VI.

Zion and I talk vampires and werewolves

he is 4 going on 127 / that's what he told me

I have no choice but to believe him

we decide we are vampires / cause / there is nothing cooler than that

we decide we don't need 2 drink blood for substance / will drink juice

Laurie offers conversation / and cabbage /

and side but full plate of sweet tasting chicken

Zion and I now trace our histories and futures

and we decide / we R going 2 break all the rules of what can kill a vampire

we create a secret handshake / Zion said

"grandma Laurie can't know it because she is not a vampire like us"

and we parlay our pact into this fang-driven world / into a fearless existence

we don't give fear space in this world of ours / and that works for both of us

Zion draws me a picture / a portrait if you will

while he bangs a beat out with his mouth / given his mother is AmberSunShower

it makes all the sense in the world to me

he nods his body / and uses his feet to the floor / 2 accent his rhythm

he nods his head to his creation like an old hip hop head from waaaaaayyyyyy

back in the day / yaheard / he asked me to help shade in the picture

we sit on the hardwood floor and I see a vision of my children back home

Zell was fighting a local virus / but through the telephone his laugh was strong

and my heart eased a little / Zion and I make a pact to record in the future

cause as Zion said / *"vamps have to stick together"*

and as a fellow vamp in the new order / what else could I say

but / *"Hell, yeah"*/ but I let the Hell dangle cause / Zion is 4

this was good company cause I'm alone a lot here

alone with the buzz of tell lies vison

most times / I don't watch / just like the fact there are other voices available

If I need them / this life / road warrior / is this for me

my children cultivate / back home / and what if I miss

what am I missing / but what am I teaching them / dreams can be captured

just like that / I'm back to my universe school / learning to release

Sharon / the living playwright left yesterday / I miss her deep seated smile

and her positivity and support / glows and radiates / off of her

sitting here in Laurie's flat / for a brief / moment / I forgot what home looks like

but I have a photo of my babies / and I am quickly reminded

I pray / 2 move / only in the direction / the universe makes for me

Zion bounces with questions and energy / he makes me remember to never forget

again / I did say he was 4 going on 127 right..?

and I have no choice but to believe him / would a fellow vampire lie?

and as I depart / evening covers me

and still / there it is / this wanting but unapproachable sky above

now speaks it says *"I have never seen an artist like this before"*

and we laugh / as I stay focused headed forward

till I am / homebound

My Heart B Beating

b beating

b

blood pulse pauses

pauses blood

In the dream I saw myself or rather my spirit

there was a sliver of a silver moon in crescent position

off its center sits a star

I reached out and touched my emotions

they bordered on forgiveness / but suggested a hostile takeover

if I were but a bird / then I would b

but in this dream / I was suggested or offered wings

and my fear of flight transported itself elsewhere

like the government responsibility to its people

and landing made me nauseous

I am green tea in the morning / some thoughts go unnoticed

so they have been unionized by my right brain

and now they fly full passenger planes

into my Twin Towers / into my Pentagon

I remember trying a Bruce Lee kick

and I split my between

now I dangle in angles / and play word games with angels

and I don't trust Gabriel / he is a poor man's Lucifer

and at the table / Jimi offers me his six string

and I ask him how he can play with fingers made of solid blocks

he smiles that Jimi Hendrix smile / braces the neckline of me

and I began 2 mumble off solos in two four time

I am here 2 b an am

am I am I to the Post Meridian

Am I A Goddamn period M

Am I

I drink from colored bottles / but don't understand

why I won't shake hands with some colored men

and if there is nothing in the night but desires

then I can construct a key with strings of yarn

to deepen the effect

and I refuse to argue with / over-privileged / under-disciplined

10- and 11-year-olds / homo sapiens / man is dangerous / I keep my 2nd brother

and he keeps me / and in the dream / I saw myself

episodically / riding along the speeding trains

I never imagined the speed of Amtrak till I was in New Jersey

the ground it speaks of blues

the ground it speaks of crossroads

the ground it speaks of Robert Johnson

the ground it speaks of rivers

and they sound like Langston Hughes

but he won't talk 2 me

he says "I profess too much profanity for poetry"

but Russell Simmons never put me on Def Poetry Jam

I am here to am

am I

I grasp at truth he dodges / he thinks I'm playing freeze tag

he laughs like my son / he laughs like my daughter

I'm out of breath

I'm out of breath / and I can't feel my toes

like I have to keep pushing this pen across the page

like I can't just write bullshit for content

like I have to rip the mic

like I have to b an artist

like I have to b a child of God

like I have to b a father

like I have to b an artist

like I have to

breathe

and my heart

my heart b beating

blood pauses

pauses blood

If I can anticipate time

then I can stay on schedule

but all remains

and my heart

my heart b

my heart b beating

b

blood pulse pauses

Zell Miller III

pauses

blood

then

morning

About the author

Zell Miller III is the inaugural Poet Laureate of Austin, Texas, an award-winning interdisciplinary theater artist, playwright, and performer whose work explores identity, culture, and the human experience.

(Photo By Ivan Miller)

Named Best Poet/Writer by the *Austin Chronicle* (2004) and inducted into the Austin Arts Hall of Fame (2017), he is a leading voice in contemporary American arts.

A nationally and internationally touring artist, he has opened for Nikki Giovanni and The Last Poets and appeared on PBS and KVUE News. Award winning instructor and has worked with youth for over 26 years.

As a playwright and director, he has created 12 full-length productions, including Chronicles of an Indigenous offspring, *My Child, My Child, My Alien Child* and *Hands Up Hoodies Down*, and is a recipient of the David Mark Cohen Playwright Award. Rooted in a jazz aesthetic, his work blends poetry, theater, and movement to spark dialogue, connection, and social change.

POETS

#MAKING

IMMORTAL

310 BROWN

.com

STREET

PUBLISHING

310brownstreet.com

@310brownstreet

www.ingramcontent.com/pod-product-compliance
Lightning Source LLC
LaVergne TN
LVHW010618100826
845148LV00014B/3015

* 9 7 9 8 9 8 8 0 5 4 0 4 7 *